Dedication

To my children, who make every day worth living: may you always have the courage to do the right thing and stay true to your morals and convictions. I hope you learn from my mistakes. I can see you are already learning to be strong, compassionate, and true to yourselves. Lastly, treat yourself just as you would treat others and never forget how amazing you are. Never forget to be a custodian of yourself and your environment.

I've written this book with the sincere desire to help anyone who has been pulled into prostitution for any reason. Everything you will read on the following pages is true, and because these things happened in my life, I can say to the man, woman, or child who recognizes a bit of him or herself in these pages - take heart. My hope is that I can give you hope. If my words and my story help you find the strength to make a change in your life, I will have met my goal.

Lastly, for everyone reading any portion of this book, I hope that you will be inspired to act more kindly toward others, be less judgmental of strangers and friends alike, and help one another's dreams come true.

Disclaimer

This book is based on true events in my life recreated from my memory, the recollections of others, and documentation. Portions are strictly my opinion and my point of view. The evidence presented in this book is subject to interpretation, speculation, conjecture, and opinion therefore readers are encouraged to explore other sources of information before reaching their own conclusions.

Some names of people, businesses, and locations have been changed to protect their safety and well being. Some information such as emails and documents have been slightly altered by omission and/or redaction to protect privacy.

As an artist, some artistic liberties have been used in the layout, organization, and style of the book that may depart from traditional vocation to make the work organic to reflect the views of the author, Shailey M. Tripp.

i

Boys Will Be Boys:

Media, Morality, and the Cover-up of the Todd Palin
Shailey Tripp Sex Scandal

Shailey M. Tripp

with Vickie Bottoms

Createspace, An amazon.com company
North Charleston, S.C.

www.createspace.com

First published by Createspace, February 16, 2012

ISBN-13: 978-1470091026
ISBN-10: 147009102X

Library of Congress Control Number: 2012903464

Table of Contents

Foreword

With pleasure

Shailey emotes every possible gamut of human emotion while employing self-deprecating humor throughout her painful odyssey in Palin's Alaska. She has learned by trying, falling, getting up and trying again.

She cannot afford the basics for herself or her children with disabilities. She endures the heartache of being alienated and homeless. Therefore she learns how "boys will be boys" behavior will afford her some monetary relief as a full service masseuse and allow her to live independently with her children. Not so with her psyche. A painful debt of self loathing and disgust follow her every time she decides to believe Todd Palin, the First Dude, (her words, Dud) and envisions he will lead her through prostitution to unknown riches and stability.

There is the subtle and the obvious in writing. Shailey uses subtleties to point to the obvious. We are surrounded by the odiousness of this livelihood and really want her to find a way out. It is difficult to imagine a more humiliating event than her imminent arrest on prostitution charges. Alaska is a cover-your-ass state. Todd Palin was going to cover his ass as "that is just the way he rolls." (Borrowing from Todd's statement about how well Sarah would deliver her Vice Presidential acceptance speech.) Did he learn that from Sarah or did Sarah ("I'll do anything I want until the courts tell me I can't") learn that from Todd?

Shailey's story may be foreign to some, if not most, readers; that does not mean it is uncommon. I once reviewed a manuscript for a former Newark, New Jersey cop. His journey was trying to rescue his teen age prostitute girlfriend from the claws of the Newark mob that ran the city. Police included. This man and his girlfriend were tortured and even his young daughter was included in the fray. The girlfriend was imprisoned and assaulted while in prison. She ended up pregnant with HIV. She died shortly after she was released.

The ex-cop ended up wandering around central Florida to stay low and try to get his message out. He disappeared before I could help him. The last time I saw him was when he came to pick up the manuscript that never got published. His eyes were grey and steely when I couldn't give him the hoped for answer for becoming published. Beyond disappointed. I got it. I was one of "them" because I did not help.

I decided after meeting Shailey, and hearing Shailey, that this travesty has not changed in the last 30 years, be it urban New Jersey or Anchorage, Alaska. This time, maybe I could help. Shailey speaks honestly and from the heart ... a good heart. I have heard the word "love" many times. Never once have I heard the word "hate".

Shailey has stepped beautifully into self-love and radiance. Her poetry refreshingly reflects: looking, smelling and feeling. The universe is obviously reflecting love back to her. I think that I am going to go light some white sage now and wrap my arms around my knees........

The real odyssey of Shailey Lawes Tripp is beginning......

Enid L. Dunn

Mother of two comics, food and garden blogger and reformed homecoming queen. Worships MFK Fisher, Dorothy Parker, Kate Hepburn, Meryl Streep and Adele. Aspiring author and person.

Lives in a Victorian and minds her own business. Mostly. Website: http://www.gardenofenid.com/

Boys Will Be Boys:

Media, Morality, and the Cover-up of the Todd Palin
Shailey Tripp Sex Scandal

Introduction

On December 11, 2011 Sarah Palin appears on Hannity with Sean Hannity, a Fox News Show, and offers her opinion on the affairs of Hermain Cain.

Transcript
(Jan. 31, 2012. http://www.foxnews.com/on-air/hannity/node/3472)

HANNITY: All right. I hope you were just listening to Herman Cain. There's a bigger issue in play here because long before the issue of sexual harassment and this most recent charge came up, he was being called all sorts of names, and the media seems to just be willing to do this and go along with this.

You have experienced this as a conservative woman. Why is — why do we live now at a time of political correctness, yet if you're a conservative, you're a woman, you're an African-American conservative, you can say anything you want, nobody seems to care?

PALIN: Yes, isn't that something? Well, we need to not be afraid of being accused of being racist just because we call out, for instance, Obama and his socialist policies, and his associations and his past record that prove that he would seek to fundamentally transform America.

We cannot be afraid of what the name calling will do to us. But yes, you're spot on when you talk about the hypocrisy and the double standards in the media.

You know in regard to Herman Cain and what he is going through, I'll tell you, Sean, in many voters' book, including mine, character counts. And if Herman Cain did not engage in this recent 13-year affair, no screwing around on his wife and giving money to some broad on the side unbeknownst to his wife, well, then, if he did not do this, then the false accuser is really despicable and we shouldn't have to put up with that kind of false accusation that results in somebody's character being so besmirched and really ruined.

HANNITY: Yes.

PALIN: If he did do it, though, Sean, if he did it, if he engaged in this recent affair and is misleading the public, then, you know, like they say, boys will be boys, but they shouldn't run the country. And it's going to be refreshing when facts come out on this so that people can make up their mind, make their own judgment on this, and then we can move on and start talking about the issues that really matter.

Coincidently three days later on December 14, 2011 an officer from the Anchorage Police Department who identified himself as Ryan from Internal Affairs calls me, Shailey Tripp. In that phone conversation Ryan let me know that my official complaint to Internal Affairs in regards of an officer's unethical and demeaning behavior towards me was trivial and would not be investigated further simply because he knew the officer, Lt. Parker, and assured me he meant no harm. Ryan, "Oh, that Parker, he can be a handful but he didn't mean any harm."

The Prologue

Why on earth isn't Kashawn answering the phone, I wondered as I pulled into the parking lot of my office complex. She had sounded very upset when she left the message on my cell phone while I was at the drive-thru buying our lunch. She said my appointment had arrived and he was angry that I was not there. She wanted to know what she should do. When I checked my messages again before leaving McDonald's there was another one letting me know that she had made the man comfortable. I could tell she was mad.

I tried to call her back at least five times on both the office phone and her cell phone. I left several messages telling her that I did not have an appointment scheduled and that she should ask the man to leave.

"If he gives you any trouble," I said, "call your boyfriend or call the police."

In my last message, I asked her why in the hell had she even let the man in. She was not supposed to let anyone enter the office when I was not present; just answer the phone.

It had been a hectic morning and I had completely forgotten to tell Kashawn about an odd call that came in on my cell phone while I was dropping my kids off at school that morning. Now I grew more worried as I remembered the call from some man who said he wanted to make an appointment for a massage. I had told him that the massage part of the business was being phased out and then I asked him who he was and how he had gotten my number. He would not identify himself. He just told me that he was referred. I said he must be mistaken because I did not take referrals. Still, he insisted that he had been referred; placing emphasis on the word *referred* and even claimed that I had stood him up twice before.

I had no idea what he was talking about but I told him to call back between noon and 1:00 p.m. and perhaps we could set up a time to meet in person to discuss the matter. He never called. The parking lot was unusually full and my frustration mounted while I circled looking for a place to park. Kashawn was not answering the phone and I was growing more and more concerned. I needed to make sure she was okay.

Finally, a space came open. I parked and ran up the stairs. I needed to check on Kashawn and I also had to use the bathroom. The office door was locked and it looked as if the lights were off. I banged on the door.

"Kashawn!" I called. "Open the door and take the food. I've got to go pee!" No answer. I waited, shifting from one foot to the other. I knocked on the door again but there was still no response. That eased my mind about Kashawn's safety. I assumed she had gotten rid of the man and left. Kashawn was a little temperamental and not answering her phone was probably her way of letting me know she was miffed.

I set the bag of food down and looked for my keys. That is when I noticed there were men all over the place. Big men. I thought they were doing construction work in the office next to mine.

One of the men approached me and started asking about the computer business. Business had been somewhat slow and I needed new clients. Lunch was forgotten. I was excited. Peeing was no longer my priority as I asked him for details about his computer problem. He inferred that Decor Lighting, a neighboring business that often sent me customers, had recommended me to him.

We chatted pleasantly for a few minutes then abruptly his whole tone and demeanor changed. He started getting in my face. He became mean. I was alarmed and felt threatened. Twice, I asked him to back off but he wouldn't. Finally, I told him I was armed and would not hesitate to defend myself. Suddenly he pulled out a pair of handcuffs and grabbed my wrists roughly. Before I could comprehend what was happening, he slapped the cuffs on me.

I was shaking now. My need to use the bathroom was totally forgotten. I was terrified. Was he going to rob me? Rape me? Kill me?

"You're a lying whore. You aren't in the computer business. This is just a front for a whorehouse and that is all you are. A whore." He must be a nut, I thought. I had seen the crime shows where serial killers targeted hookers. My mouth went dry with fear and my heart raced.

Then unexpectedly my office door opened and he pushed me inside. He asked if I was the owner, Tia. I told him I was the owner but my name was Shailey. Then he produced a copy of my lease and said I had rented the office to run a computer business but the girl in the office had solicited an officer for sex. That is when I realized what was going on. A police raid.

Kashawn was handcuffed behind her desk. She was only eighteen and her big brown eyes were wide with fear. The other officers present instructed her not to speak to me. For over an hour, they yelled at me and grilled me. Whom did I see in my office? Important people? They already knew who they were. Name them and all this would go away. By this point, time had no meaning to me. The officers were getting really angry. I did not cry or talk. I was in a state of shock.

One officer was introduced to me and I was told this was his bust. I asked him his name and when he spoke, I looked closer. Officer Padgett. He was a former client of mine. A sexual client. Then I noticed two F.B.I. agents there who were also former clients. No way in hell was I going to say anything now. I knew this was serious business.

My need to use the restroom had returned. I asked them if I could be excused. I also reminded them that Kashawn and I had not eaten yet, even though the thought of food made me nauseous. What I really wanted was some time to think without them harassing me. They let me go to the bathroom located in the outside hallway, but they sent an officer in with me. A male officer.

He told me he was going to search the bathroom for condoms before I would be allowed to relieve myself. He also informed me that the reason they were there was because the police had received two complaint calls from other tenants in the building and that before I got back they had searched the women's bathroom and found over fifty used douche bottles in the trash can. Those bottles, he said, would be their cause for arresting me.

My first thought was this was the most idiotic thing I had ever heard. Douche bottles? Really? I wondered how they could arrest me based on finding used douche bottles in a semi-public bathroom. Any number of people could have used these facilities. I started to ask the officer just that but decided against saying anything.

After about five minutes or so, the officer said he was through looking. I did not know if he found anything or not. I had zoned out while he was searching, wondering what was coming next.

The toilet was located in a stall so at least I was allowed privacy while I emptied my bladder. I was warned not to flush the toilet. I do not know what they thought they were going to find but I really wish that I could have taken a crap!

I was escorted back to the office. They said we could have our lunch now but took Kashawn in another room to eat. The burger was dry and the fries stale but I ate, chewing slowly, while I tried to think. I could not believe all this was really happening. I was going to need someone to pick up my kids from school and look after them if I was arrested. Would the police let me make a call?

After about fifteen minutes, they threw away the remaining food and brought Kashawn back into the room. I was told three different stories about Kashawn getting busted for prostitution. They told me I needed to tell the truth for her sake. Still I said nothing. Finally, they gave up and took Kashawn behind a partitioned wall. They said they were turning off the tape recorder. They told her to cooperate if she knew what was good for her.

"So Kashawn, you said earlier you were going to give a massage to Officer Peters and then he asked what else you did and you offered sex for money. Is that correct?" She said yes. Then they tried very hard to get her to say I was involved with sex trafficking and was keeping her as a sex slave but she would not go that far. So they told her that they knew all about her and her arrest record. They said they knew she was pregnant and if she knew what was good for her she needed to get her story straight and follow their lead. They told her word for word what to say and told her if she testified against me her record would be clean and she would go free.

Finally, they let her leave but took all her personal belongings from her. She was upset and crying. We gave each other looks as she left. Not mean ones, in my opinion, just of concern. The officer in charge of the task force, the one who was my former client, Padgett, never looked at me and never asked me any questions. At one point, the officer questioning me asked if I knew anyone in the room and I said no.

I could only think about my kids and about telling Richard. What was Richard going to say? Telling Richard I had been arrested was the worst thing I could think of; it loomed very large in my thoughts, crowding out other things.

My private musings were interrupted when an officer asked about Todd Palin. I was asked if he had ever been in my office and had he been a client. I said yes. Everyone in the room started to act weird at this point. The officer questioning me pressed on about how they knew Todd saw me frequently. He said that neighbors in the building reported that they often saw him come to my office and leave; claiming they heard many loud and inappropriate noises that sounded like sex noises whenever he was present. I just gave the man a look that I hoped conveyed that I thought he was an idiot.

Many times Richard told me about the corruption of the police and advised me never to say anything at all if I was ever arrested for anything. I had already noted what they did with Kashawn, not having things recorded. Richard's words rang in my head. I decided not to say too much more. I don't know why I ever said anything at all. Probably because I had never been so scared in my life. At one point, even though they did not have a search warrant yet, I offered them a notebook. I told them that it was our note book of all the sinister people with whom I refused to have sex.

I offered it hoping they might go easier on

me if I cooperated, but it did not work. They would not even look at it. They asked a lot of questions about clients' names, if there were drugs and guns present, and if I knew anything about sex trafficking of young girls. They seemed most interested in the names of clients.

Once they realized I was not going to talk and they did not find any contraband, they seemed to be confused and had to regroup. They told me they were going to take me in and book me. Right before they took me away I was allowed to make a call. Thank God, I was worried about my kids. I called Richard. He assured me he would take care of the kids and arrange to have me bailed out. I could hear the hurt and concern in his voice. That is when the reality of my situation hit me. What had I done?

The ride to the police station seemed to last forever yet it was over all too soon. The Anchorage Police Department holding jail is located in a large brick building. The driver went around to the back where a door opened and we drove inside. Everything about the interior seemed to be concrete – cold and unmovable.

We were not alone. There were other officers waiting with the people they had arrested. It looked like a scene from a movie. It did not seem real, adding to that feeling of disbelief I had. We went inside and one of the officers had to speak into an intercom to say they had brought me in. We had to wait quite a while in the hallway with the others waiting to be processed. All men. I kept thinking I do not belong here.

Finally, they took me inside around 4:00 p.m. Things kept getting more and more bizarre. While going through booking, I saw an officer who had been a legitimate massage client of mine and two uniformed men present had been sexual clients. Add to this the two F.B.I. agents who were sexual clients, and two other people who were my friends, all in the booking area.

One of these friends had worked with me at a spa that was part of a women's clinic. She was shocked to see me there and appalled at the charge. I wondered if they planned my arrest to coincide with a time when my friends would be working just to embarrass me. They searched me, had me empty my pockets, waved the wand over and around me, and fingerprinted me. At some point they read me my Miranda rights, photographed me and had me sign for the belongings they took.

I felt humiliated. I hoped to never experience anything like this again. Officer Padgett never once looked me in the eye nor spoke to me during this entire time. It made me very uneasy. Then I was led through a door that opened into yet another large room. The floor was concrete. On the left was a huge bar and the officers were sitting behind it. A television was on and I noticed two old fashioned pay phones.

I was directed to sit down and not speak to anyone. I went to a corner, lowered myself onto the uncomfortable seating, pulled my knees up to my chest and buried my head in my hands. How had I gotten to this point? Immediately, my memory presented me with images from a day in

2006; the day I first met Todd Palin.

BIG

Basking, waiting patiently
In the beats of the sun
Gaining time
Building our foundation
Instant trust
Gilded in bronze
Besides myself with angst
Intrinsic tapping of my foot
Growing in love.

©Shailey M Lawes

Chapter One

Fall 2006

At thirty two years of age, I was at the lowest point in my life. Or so I thought. Already under my belt I had two failed marriages, a foreclosed home, various physical illnesses, and long periods of unemployment. In addition, I was a single mom with two small children; both were still in diapers, both were disabled, and I had miscarried a set of twins. Adding to my problems was the domestic violence with both my second husband and my father. My second husband, Jimmy, tried to poison the kids and me. Surviving almost being killed and watching my kids get attacked rounded out the picture of my life as a woman, a wife, and a mom. Then after I left that situation I walked into my father's world of extreme control and him turning the whole family against me. I know this sounds cliché but, my life story would have made a great plot for a soap opera.

As I said, if anyone had told me that things were going to get any worse, I would not have believed it possible. But something began taking root in the fall of 2006 that became more hurtful to me than any of the aforementioned challenges, losses, and burdens. Something I never would have believed myself capable of, something truly awful.

In 2004 as my second marriage began to come to an end, I gathered up the children and moved from Alabama to Alaska to live with my parents. This pattern I repeated three more times. I should have made a clean break right then and there, if I had things might have been different, but instead, when my husband begged me to come back, I did. After only a few months in Alaska, I packed up the kids and went back to him. In total, it took me nine times of going back to him before I had finally left him for good. This yo-yo process enraged my family and added to them thinking I was crazy. When I was pregnant with my son and went back to Jimmy one final time - the ninth time - it was a miracle I escaped him alive! I believe firmly had I not left my children would be dead. This will sound incredible, but I wanted so badly for him to love me that nothing else mattered. As a result, I put my daughter, Salora and my son, Brice, in a dangerous situation. Sick, I know.

Jimmy tried to rape me in front of my daughter, then he tried to kill all of us through poisoning our drinks. That's what it took for me to finally leave. Luckily, the police helped us get an angel flight out of the area and advised me to never come back. I took their advice and haven't looked back.

The children and I returned to my parents' home in Alaska and it was then I discovered I was pregnant with twins. I also discovered that my parents had paid a detective large sums of money to follow me around while I was in Alabama. It wasn't for our protection, it was to build a case to take my children away from me. In addition to this my Mom and Dad were very controlling and wanted me to live under rules that felt suffocating to me. No wonder my paranoia and stress levels soared.

My family did not feel it was their place to help me raise my children. They had paid their dues and wanted other things in life and did not feel their hard earned money should have to be used to help me raise my kids. When they began to see the high medical needs of the kids and how much time it took they began to pressure me to give them up for adoption. Once I told them I was pregnant they insisted I put the unborn babies up for adoption.

I was being reminded constantly that I could barely manage the two children that were already here. The stress of all that, plus having to work and contribute to the household finances, proved too much for me. I suffered a miscarriage. It was beyond devastating, but deep down I believed I deserved it; I knew God wanted me to suffer. And for the next five years suffer I did.

I went into a deep depression after I lost the twins. I think my depression was part post-partum, part the loss of my unborn children, and part the long healing process involved in leaving an abusive relationship, and handling the mental adjustment of having handicapped children. But I can only see that now when I look back. To this day many people do not give me grace or even just an understanding of what this period of time was like for me. That used to bother me. But now I have a sense of peace but this peace did not come easy and I paid a high price for it.

However at that moment I was a mess, my emotions all over the place. I was obsessive about caring for my two children. Family and friends didn't understand. They told me I was lazy and worthless. On top of all that, I had my father and my ex-husband telling me I was crazy or bi-polar, that I wasn't a good mom, that I was ungrateful, that I was causing everyone financial stress, anything negative - you name it, they said it. I believed every word. The real truth was that I was a good person who was going through a bad time. But when my dad began saying it, too, I internalized it and believed it and lived it.

I became suspicious of everyone. My father and I were arguing constantly. Eventually things came to a head and my dad kicked us out of the house. My children and I went to a shelter. Shelter life is hard enough when your kids are healthy. Trying to cope with two disabled children in that environment was almost impossible. I couldn't get a job because I had to care for the kids. At one point, I thought I was going to have to give my children up to the state.

One day my Mom came to the shelter. I thought she was going to take us to the store. Instead, she handed me an envelope. I begged her to take me to get some diapers. She refused and informed me that no one in our family would help me anymore. She was only there to deliver a message. She said, "Read the letter."

The envelope was labeled "When you are ready to take the first step" and it contained a list of all my wrongdoings and demands that I had to meet before I would receive any further assistance from my family. That letter broke my heart. Especially the fact that my brother, who I had practically raised, had signed it. My parents were the leaders among our extended family and they used their influence to turn all of them against me.

(Letter)
Dearest Daughter,

This is a declaration of unacceptable behavior that will not be tolerated within the family. This is not a negotiation. You have hurt yourself, your children, and the people around you by making false accusations about your family to others. Some of these accusations have been made directly; some through insinuation. Your family has welcomed you and your children with loving, open arms with the intent of helping you to restore physical, mental, spiritual and financial health. You have only repaid these acts of love with hatred, resentment and manipulation. What you have done to your children and to us is reprehensible.

You have tossed your family aside, as one would only throw away a piece of trash. To you, we are expendable. Your children are bonded to us; but you bring to your children un-necessary and cruel separation of bereavement for their

grandparents. Overall, you have hurt yourself, your children, and the people around you. You have specifically done the following:
- not provide proper medical care to your child
- have falsely accused and spread rumors about your father of (redacted)
- have placed your children and yourself in violent domestic circumstance
- have removed your children from a stable, permanent, and loving home;
- have lied to family members about various subjects
- have allowed your temper and attitude to become uncontrolled and unacceptable
- have not shown gratitude toward people who are helping you;
- have found ways to alienate people who care about you
- have continuing episodes of depression that has lasted longer than a year and have not sought help for it
- have used your children to hurt your family
- have misplaced unresolved anger toward your family.

You have placed us in an awkward situation. We, as family, are no longer able to help you, because helping you places our physical, mental, spiritual and financial health in danger. In order for us to help you the following must be done:
1. Written, notarized recant for falsely accusing your father of (redacted), of being a threat to both your children.

2. Written, notarized recant for falsely accusing your mother for inappropriately grand parenting your children.

3. A verbal, public apology to both of your parents in a group of your parents' choosing. This apology is for the above false accusations.

4. Participation in family healing to include your father, your mother, your brother and yourself. This is to be conducted by a healer of your parents choice. This shall be a minimum of six sessions. Walking out of a session or disrupting a session nulls and voids that session.

5. Proof that you have submitted yourself to a comprehensive, diagnostic assessment to include spiritual, psychosocial and physical aspects by a licensed and experienced professional in mental health. An advocate of your choice who is considered a respected healer by the community will present a written summary of that assessment to your father, your mother, your brother. That healer will have your written consent to discuss your needs thoroughly with your family.

Until you have complied, we will not aid you and we will not comfort you. Know that until you can admit there is something wrong with you, you are robbing yourself and your children of the healing they deserve. What is stated here is a declaration, not a negotiation.

Hope and love,

Your family. Mom, Dad, Brother.

Most of the charges in the letter were reflective of my father's point of view. From my perspective, he was wrong and he was the one out of control. He made it seem as if I had lied to our family when, in truth, he was the one who lied to our family. He made me look so bad that no one in my family wanted anything to do with me. The worst consequence of this was a couple years later when my grandfather died I never got to talk to him. Grandad would not even accept letters from me and had them returned in the mail. When he passed away I was devastated, and I never even got to tell him that I loved him.

I can't say that I was completely innocent of all the charges mentioned in the letter. I had endangered my kids. I had and still suffered from depression. Who wouldn't become depressed under those circumstances? However, I wasn't as ungrateful as they claimed, nor were my parents perfect themselves. How dare they ostracize me? I showed the letter to my counselor at the shelter, who then told the shelter authorities about it. I was informed that the letter was considered a form of domestic violence and that my family was committing abuse against me because of the list of demands in that letter. I was also told that victims of domestic violence weren't allowed in that particular shelter and that we would have to leave there soon. I had only shared the letter with my counselor in hopes of getting some insight from an unbiased third party so that I might deal appropriately with my family's actions toward me. Once again, something bad had come from my efforts to do something good.

A few days later my kids and I were forced to leave the shelter. We were told we really belonged in a domestic violence shelter and in any case they weren't equipped to handle children with disabilities. We could come there for counseling and an evening meal but we could no longer live there. When I asked if they could transfer us to a domestic violence shelter, I was told the nearest one was full.

The kids and I ended up spending a few nights in a public restroom. It was uncomfortable but anything was better than being on the street. Fall is cold in Alaska. We returned to the shelter each day for meals and counseling. My pride almost made me not go but I had to for the children's sake. I had no other way to feed them. Then one of the counselors at the shelter gave me the telephone number for Family Promise, an organization that helps homeless people get a fresh start. I decided to call and I was asked to come in for an interview. I was nervous during the session with the intake counselor and I was sure that they wouldn't be able to help us. But when the kids and I went to the shelter the next day to eat, someone from Family Promise was there waiting for us. We had been accepted into their program.

The Family Promise program was very different from what I had been used to at my parents' home. I wasn't criticized or judged. And, no one was telling me when to eat, when to sleep, and when to play with my kids. There were rules, of course, but there was also lots of encouragement, hot meals, a safe place, and, most importantly, the space I needed to be myself and make plans for the future. In six weeks time, I turned my life around.

With references from Family Promise and my credentials, I was hired as a substitute teacher for the Mat-Su Valley School System. I subbed for teachers, monitors, and even crossing guards at whichever school needed me on any given day. I also had a second job as a massage therapist at Bonnie's Spa. Bonnie was willing to schedule massage appointments around my assignments with the school system.

I was able to get an apartment for us but furniture

had to wait. The kids and I slept on blankets and padding on the hardwood floor. Transportation was a big challenge. With no car, we had to leave at 5:00 a.m. in order to catch the bus that took the kids to daycare and me to work. Some days we spent four to five hours on the bus. Family Promise did help with arranging transportation to the kids' medical appointments but most of the time getting to where we needed to be was nerve wracking.

Still, our lives were much better than they had been. Then Todd Palin entered my life. My first meeting with Todd was purely by chance. It was a few days before Thanksgiving. I was assigned to Wasilla Middle School that week and my duties the first day were making sure that the kids went to class and supervising the kids in the lunchroom and the gym.

Kids like to see what they can get away with when a new monitor is on duty. On this particular day that is exactly what happened, some kids decided to cut in front of the line and make a game of it. The servers and the women collecting money scolded them. The girls talked back to the staff in an ugly way, so I went over and made them go to the back of the line. As soon as I turned my back, they tried it again. I made them go to the rear once more, this time not taking my eyes off them.

After lunch I had to unlock the gymnasium and supervise the kids while they played basketball. While I was getting the basketballs from a locked closet, the girls who were cutting up in the lunchroom came in. They started whining about not having a ball. I offered them one. One girl got in my face and complained that I was picking on them and wouldn't let them play. She was very rude to me so I put her in what I call "time out." The school calls it "take a step" and "step two" is the same as a time out. I knew my options; I could give her detention, send her to the office or send a note home to her parents. I chose to send a note home.

As a monitor I didn't have a list of the students' names. If I were to ask the girl who she was, I would have no way of knowing if she was telling the truth or not, so I simply wrote the note describing her behavior and addressed it "To Whom It May Concern." I handed it to the girl and told her to give it to her parents. I thought she would throw it away. I probably would have when I was her age.

The next day I was in the office talking with one of the officers who came to the school every afternoon. As the officer was leaving he said "Hi" to a well-dressed, nice looking man. The man was chatting with the office staff in a friendly manner. I gathered from the conversation that he was waiting for his kid to come to the office. He mentioned getting a note and the monitor's name. *My name.* I spoke up and said that I was Shailey Tripp. He introduced himself as Todd Palin and we talked for a bit.

Todd told me he worked on the Slope (the Alaskan oil fields) and that he usually picked his kids up from school when he was home. He told me he and his wife had four children. I told him I was a single mother with two kids and that I also worked as a massage therapist at Bonnie's Spa. I gave him one of my business cards with the address of the spa. It also had my email address on it. He put the card in his pocket. Todd Palin seemed like a normal parent genuinely concerned about his daughter's behavior. When the girl came into the office he made her apologize. She seemed sincere.

The following weekend I was helping out at a gambling party, which I did occasionally to make some extra money. Todd was there and he said hello to me. I remembered then that I had seen him there before. I hadn't recognized him at the school because he had been dressed up. The gambling affairs were hosted by a couple at their home on a local lake and the guests were encouraged to dress in casual, comfortable attire. My duties were to give neck and shoulder massages at the tables, help with serving dinner and drinks and serve as a "gofer." If anything was needed from the store or a guest wanted something special, I got it for them. The guests were important people and their hosts spared no expense to make sure they were happy.

One of the other helpers clued me in to the fact that Todd was the husband of a woman who was going to be Governor of Alaska. I know it sounds strange but I had no idea who the Palins were. I guess it was a combination of being fairly new to the area and a lack of interest in politics. Truth be told, I was so tired from working and taking care of Salora and Brice, I seldom watched the news or read the newspaper. So I wasn't really impressed by Mrs. Palin's political ambitions or that the man I met was connected in that way. In fact, I translated "going to be Governor" as "running for" instead of "incumbent." I didn't even know the elections had taken place. Politics had no place in my busy, stress-filled life.

The next week I was surprised to see Todd's name on my massage schedule. At the time, I thought it was a good thing. My Family Promise counselor had suggested my giving a business card to every new acquaintance I made because they might become a client. When I saw his name I was happy that her advice seemed to be working. The first massage I gave him was completely professional. Low key. We chatted about mundane things like people who are barely acquainted do; I can't remember anything in particular we discussed. I expected him to mention seeing me at the gambling party but he didn't. I do remember encouraging him to come back and asked him to recommend me to his family and friends.

As he was leaving I heard Bonnie, my boss, tell him that all of us liked to eat breakfast at Bee's, a bakery nearby. The local shop owners never missed an opportunity to plug each other's businesses.

The next morning I received an email from Todd. It was polite. He said it was nice to meet me and he thanked me for my time. A couple of days later I was at Bee's getting coffee to take back to the spa when Todd came in. He spotted me and asked if I would like to grab a bite to eat. I said yes. I had some time to kill before my first appointment. I thought making friends with someone as well-connected as Todd Palin would be a good move. Perhaps he would refer his family and friends to me, which would be wonderful because I needed to build up a base of regular clients.

He ordered a Danish and I had a croissant. We both drank coffee. Talking to him was easy but I didn't mention how hard things had been for me lately. I wanted him to see me as a successful professional woman. We talked for about fifteen minutes. He mentioned that he needed a tie for an upcoming event and that he didn't like shopping. We talked for a few more minutes, then he glanced at his watch. He said he'd just remembered there was somewhere he needed to be. He asked if I would mind paying the check. I didn't really have the money to spare but I didn't want to admit it so I said, "Of course not."

Monday of the next week I was checking my schedule for the next day and saw Todd's name on the list again. I was glad for the repeat business. He must have liked my services, or so I thought. I remembered him saying he needed a tie and I just happened to have a couple that I had picked up for a friend. They were nice silk ties that I had gotten on sale so I decided to give one to Todd. It was just a friendly gesture to build goodwill between us. I figured a man like Todd Palin could refer many wealthy people to me and the money I spent would be returned many times over.

During the second massage I was more relaxed with Todd. I let down my guard a little and admitted that at times I was overwhelmed by my responsibilities. He told me to stay calm and let things take care of themselves. He seemed pleased when I gave him the tie.

The afternoon of the day he came for the second massage I emailed Todd to thank him for his advice about staying calm. I also told him that I thought we should keep our friendship and professional relationship separate. I really felt somewhat weird about how close we were getting in such a short time. I also told him not to sweat breakfast, even thought if he'd read between the lines and applied what he now knew of my troubles, he would have understood that was my reminding him that he owed me money. Maybe he did understand, but it wasn't enough to prompt him to repay me.

He replied to my email in less than an hour. He said that he was happy to be there for me, that he was glad we had met, and added, "you light up my life." That was a bit jarring. He also said he loved the tie.

To put Todd Palin's actions into context, this email he sent me was dated December 5, 2006. He was emailing with me, promptly and flirtatiously, the day after his wife took the oath of office. Governor Sarah Palin started her term as governor of the State of Alaska on December 4 and the First Dude was quoting and old Debbie Boone song to me less than twenty-four hours later. The date meant nothing to me at the time, as I've said, politics wasn't part of my life. But it has been pointed out to me since then that he must have thought that being friendly and encouraging me, a single mom with a lot of problems, was going to pay off in ways much more valuable to him than another Danish with coffee.

I liked Todd but I didn't have any romantic feelings toward him. I just wanted to be friends with him because I thought it would be good for my business. I see now that the intimate tone of that email should have given me a warning about what was coming next, but I was clueless. My naiveté didn't last long.

Rain,

The dim light withers,
the rain brings shivers
Lightning flashes,
thunder clashes
Rain pours down
The world turns calm
Fears, tears, disease, and poverty washed
away
A war of lightning holds the world still
The clouds grow dark in fiery anger
And the wind dances and sings in an
ailing cry
Down pours the rain
Washing away...

© Shailey Lawes

Chapter Two

It was the middle of December. My life was hectic working for the school system, the spa, and occasionally moonlighting at the gambling parties; not to mention life in general, medical appointments, getting therapy for my children, paying the bills, and the family tensions that always seem to spring up during the holidays.

Yet, when I worked at the spa in Wasilla, I always felt joy and a connection to my community. The spa work gave me some relief from my stresses. My co-workers were positive influences on my life. The clients made me feel good about myself, too. They made me feel important and needed.

Bonnie used to be the Palin's hairdresser. She was the best in the area and well respected by her clients so I wasn't at all surprised when I found out that she knew Todd. Once in a while, he came into the shop, and he and Bonnie would be cordial, catching up with one another the way old high school friends do. They'd talk about his fishing, his work with BP, the local weather. They would share stories about their children and empathize with each other about the challenges of parenthood. They discussed the things most people talk about with their hairdresser. However, she wasn't cutting his hair; he was just dropping by to say hello. At least that's the way Todd wanted it to appear. Later, I would understand it was more than that. It wasn't genuine. He was laying the groundwork. It was a way to gain my trust without speaking directly to me. In fact, these couple of times he came by the spa, he didn't speak to me at all.

Bonnie was so personable and people loved her so much that Todd knew it would be easy for me to believe in their friendship. He knew I would trust him because he was a friend of Bonnie's. He used Bonnie and deceived us both.

I had little spare time between all my jobs, and what I did have was spent with my children. The holidays were coming and I really wanted them to be extra special that year. Salora was three and Brice was two-both of them just old enough to be excited about Santa Claus and his upcoming visit to our house. We had been living in our little apartment in Palmer for about three weeks and I felt that I needed to make up to them for us having been homeless. I wanted to give them lots of Christmas surprises. But, barring a miracle, there would be few presents under the tree Christmas morning-if I were even able to get a tree.

The week before Christmas, Todd came into the spa. It was nearly closing time. He asked me if I had time to give him a massage. I said yes I did. In the back of my mind, I was hoping he would give me a nice tip or maybe purchase gift certificates from me to give as Christmas presents. Perhaps he would refer some other people to me and I would be able to get some extra gifts for the kids after all.

Allowing myself to believe that this was an answer to my Christmas needs, I probably had a happy smile and a glow of anticipation. But it wasn't about the client Todd Palin, it was joy stemming from the thought that this Christmas would be a good one, and the upcoming year held promise because having Todd Palin as a client could lead to more clients that could grow to provide a decent income and a decent life for my children and me. I wouldn't have to give Salora and Brice up to the state for adoption. In that moment, I could see a way to keep them, and raise them, and be the mother they needed me to be. I must have lit up like a Christmas tree. How could I not?

Therefore, there was no way I would have said no and this was going to be the best massage Todd Palin ever had; we went through the usual preparations prior to the massage. I went over the medical forms verbally, just to make sure nothing had changed since last time. Everything seemed fine. I told him, as I do all my male massage clients, to dress down and keep his underwear on. I instructed Todd to lie on the table, face up or face down, and cover with the blanket. I left the room and gathered the supplies while he disrobed.

My table was a really good one that I kept warm with a heating pad underneath. It helped my clients relax, and I found they really appreciated this extra touch, especially when they had come in from the cold.

When I returned, Todd lay face up and I began to massage him exactly the same way I had the two previous times. I expected he would be quiet during the massage except for an occasional instruction or a little small talk. That was how it went both times before. To my surprise, right away, Todd began making moaning noises and he kept telling me how tense he was. He was much more into the massage this time.

Suddenly, he grabbed hold of my hand. My first thought was that I might have hit a tender spot. I started to apologize but before I could say anything, he placed my hand on his penis-his bare, *erect* penis! I was shocked and started to jerk my hand away. But he squeezed it to keep me from moving it. He asked me if I would mind helping him out with his "problem." He said there would be a little something extra in it for me if I would take care of it.

It was an awful moment. The choices were between doing something for Todd Palin that I did not want to do in order to have the money to play Santa for Salora and Brice, or refusing to degrade myself while knowing there would be little, if anything, under the tree for the children on Christmas morning.

I dearly wanted my children to have what other kids had. I'd felt like such a bad mother. Continuing to fail my children was the worst thing I could do. And, I had already

heard their delighted squeals in the Christmas morning
preview playing over and over in my own imagination.
I know I should have said no and walked away. But in my
state of need I asked myself what harm would it really do?
It was just a hand job.

While I was stroking his erection in an up and down
motion, Todd kept making grunting sounds. He told me
how good it felt and how perfect I was, in a reassuring tone.
I think he could sense how nervous I was. After he
climaxed, he immediately became businesslike. He asked
for some tissues so he could clean himself. He dressed and
put the used Kleenex in one of his pockets. He thanked me
for the release in the impersonal way one might thank a
server, handed me fifty dollars and left. He didn't even say,
"Merry Christmas."

Words cannot explain how I felt, or what I was
thinking after Todd left. I just stood there mortified for a
long time, dumbfounded in disbelief at what had just
happened. One of the other girls finally came into the room
to see if anything was wrong. I made as if I was just
straightening up my space before leaving.

For days, I was convinced that everyone in the shop
knew what had happened even though the massage room
was isolated from the rest of the salon and the walls were
well insulated. I kept expecting Bonnie to confront me
about the incident. I was relieved when the spa closed for
Christmas.

I blamed myself. I must have been too friendly
with him. I must have sent him the wrong signals. I even
asked a couple of friends of mine who were also massage
therapists what they would do, hypothetically, in such a
situation. After mulling it over, I emailed Todd and told
him that I could no longer see him as a client. He came by
the spa and told me how sorry he was in person. He took all
the blame and assured me that nothing sexual would ever
happen again. He was a smooth talker and seemed so

sincere that stupidly, I believed him.

The New Year arrived. Todd called me once and emailed me a couple of times. I was polite but reserved when I spoke to him. I really wished he would just leave me alone, but one day he showed up at the spa again. To understand why I did what I did next you have to know the circumstances my children and I were in at the time. I was working for both the school system and the spa. I had just found out that Brice was completely deaf and Salora was still having seizures. I was trying to get Salora into physical therapy for her arm, which had been paralyzed at the time of her birth due to a botched delivery by vacuum extraction. I had started taking her to an early intervention program, which was quite a distance from where we lived. I was in counseling for domestic violence myself and transportation to all of our appointments was a challenge.

We were dependent on the public bus system for the most part, and sometimes volunteers provided rides. On top of that, there were problems at the daycare the kids were attending. My son and daughter were being bullied and picked on and the woman that operated the facility lied to me about it. I wanted to move them to a different childcare center but I didn't have the money. I couldn't ask my parents for help because we still weren't speaking. We had tried to reconcile just before Christmas but it was a disaster. Finally, I swallowed my pride and asked anyway. As I expected, they refused.

A good night's sleep was impossible to obtain. My daughter had night terrors and my son would crawl in bed with me. When I was home, they were super clingy and I didn't deal with that well. Even going to my counseling sessions was stressful because my kids had to accompany me. The saying "there's no rest for the weary" must have been coined by someone like me. We were on every public assistance program for which we were eligible but it was still one day at a time for us. It seemed as if everything I

40

did, every single decision I made, led to another series of challenges and disasters. I felt like crap. However, I also felt determined that I was going to make it and my children and I would stay together.

It was this determination to get ahead and provide a decent life for my kids that led me to make a profound, life-changing, decision, one that ultimately led me down a path of immorality and law-breaking behavior. I became a criminal.

My first instinct was to leave when he came through the door that day in January, but he sounded sincere when he promised to keep things professional and with my finances in the state they were in, I couldn't afford to turn away a client. Not even if the client was Todd Palin.

For the first ten minutes or so, the massage was completely normal. Todd was very quiet. I began to relax thinking everything was going to be okay. Then, he moaned. He asked me if I wanted to make some extra money. I wanted to refuse, but I needed money badly. I asked myself, was another hand job such a big deal? I decided it wasn't. Then, he surprised me by asking me to take off my shirt and bra. He said that he wanted to see my breasts and that he bet they were big and beautiful. Reluctantly, I did as he asked, then I asked him if he wanted me to resume the massage. He said yes and I thought that maybe my being topless was all that he would ask of me.I was wrong.

After a few minutes, he asked if he could touch my breasts. When I didn't say anything he said he would make it worth my while. I couldn't bring myself to speak so I nodded my consent. He rubbed my breasts and he commented on how round and firm they were. He said he liked "big tits." It got worse. He asked me to straddle him and rub his penis with my breasts. I did. After a while, he rolled me over and got on top of me. He pushed my breasts together with his hands, stuck his penis between them and

41

began thrusting. Humiliation, confusion and disillusion swirled inside my head. He asked if he could ejaculate on my face. I told him no. I was not going to submit to that indignity, too. He begged and offered me more money but I still refused. I told him absolutely not. No way. He climaxed in his hand and asked me if I would like to taste it. I didn't even answer. What a pervert he is, I thought. While he was cleaning himself, he asked questions. Did I like his penis? Was it normal? Wasn't it big? Had I ever seen one like his before? I gave him the answers that I thought he wanted to hear. If I had been truthful, I would have told him that his penis was strange. It was rather small and I had never seen one that was two different colors. He dressed, put the tissues in his pocket again, paid me and left. I felt terrible about the whole thing, and I sincerely hoped I had seen the last of him.

The rest of January and February passed with no sign of Todd. There were no phone calls and no emailed apologies. I was glad. I just wanted him to leave me alone. March came. My kids and I were still struggling. There was no one in my family who would speak to me except for a dying aunt. I was worn out from working two jobs and having to depend on public transportation. The kids' health problems were ongoing and I was having medical problems myself. I knew I needed to see a doctor but the thought of trying to arrange transportation to yet another appointment was more than I could handle. I even had thoughts of placing my children in foster care for a while until I could do a better job of providing for them but I couldn't bear to do it.

The first week of March, I had just finished a massage and was getting ready to leave the spa when the door opened and Todd walked in. If I'd seen him first, I'd have hidden in the back out of sight, but he had already spotted me.

He came up to me and nonchalantly asked if I had

time to give him a massage. I wanted to say no but the same internal struggle started inside me. I was trying to save up enough money to buy a used car. How could I refuse a client when I needed the money so badly, and besides, the other girls in the shop were watching and I knew they would question me if I refused him. I didn't want to have to answer their questions, I told myself, and I nodded and motioned for him to go to the massage area.

To my surprise, the massage was completely normal. He was quiet the whole time. I thought that he had finally realized the requests he had made of me before were wrong. When the massage finished without becoming sexual, I was relieved. I made my normal, professional parting comments and started to leave the room, but Todd asked me to wait.

He grabbed my arm a little forcefully and rolled over to show me how hard his penis had become. His pants were draped across a chair, and he went to them and took out his wallet. Then he held out two one hundred dollar bills and a condom. He told me the money was mine if I would ride him.

I stood there quietly for a minute, thinking, "No! Don't do this. It's wrong." That must have been the angel on one shoulder, trying to convince me not to listen to the devil whispering in my other ear, because I also had the thought, "Two hundred dollars! That, plus my regular fee will be enough for the down payment on that used car I saw a couple of days ago."

The thought that I would no longer have to wake my kids up at 4:00 a.m. every weekday morning to catch the bus was enough to make me go against my better judgment. I took off my clothes.

As I mounted him, he told me that he was a bad boy and that I had to punish him. While I was riding him, he said that I was "so tight" and that he wanted "to taste my sweet center." To escape reality, I zoned out and forced my self to think about things like grocery shopping, errands I needed to run, and calls I had to return. I just mentally removed myself from being at that place, in that situation, and with that person. I occupied my mind with mundane thoughts of everyday life. Believe me, I got no pleasure from the sexual act I entered into with the governor's husband.

As soon as he finished Todd acted as if nothing had happened. He asked for a wet washcloth with which to clean himself. I got it for him. When he got through, he tied a knot in the used condom, wrapped it in the washcloth and stuffed everything in one of his coat pockets. As he was going out the door, he said he would be in touch with me. In hindsight, I believe he was formulating plans for my future even as he zipped himself up that day. If I had known then what I know now, I would have avoided further contact with him like the plague. Instead, I was drawn deeper and deeper into what I came to realize too late was a path leading to my own destruction. Todd Palin was not the soft - spoken nice guy, friend of Bonnie, client of Shailey Tripp that he presented to the world. The reality was on the other side of my massage room door, he was a predator, and I was in his crosshairs.

Ripples

Yesterday's shadows are
bursting roads which
found my reflection
to be wiser, stronger
with time, as an edge
his might distorted
in hot waters immersed
in familiar tears
waiting. Time distorted
thoughts delicious
desires are ripples
slowly moving,
trying to stop.

©Shailey Lawes

Chapter Three

Spring 2007

The changing of the season brought many changes to my life as well. A van had been donated to Family Promise and the organization gave it to me. It was a huge relief being able to transport my son and daughter to all of their appointments without either having to be on the bus all day or asking someone for a ride. Still, I had problems both personal and financial that were not going to be solved easily.

My son had ear surgery, which allowed him to hear for the first time. That was truly a blessing but I had to be out of work for two weeks as he went through a very difficult time. He cried almost constantly due to being in pain, not to mention the strangeness to him of hearing sounds he had never heard before.

Also around this time I finally found my place in the religious community. I was baptized into the Church of Latter Days Saints in early April. This marked a passage for me spiritually. From this point on I began to see my way clearer in my search towards God and my own sense of well being. The seed was planted with the baptism. The habits and strength grew over time but in the end, gave me the foundation of strength to reach deep within myself to change my life. At the time I had no idea the importance of this commitment to faith I was making. But for me it felt right. As the Dali Lama would say I found my hat.

I was concerned about the future the kids and I were facing. School would be out soon and we would be solely dependent on my income as a massage therapist. I was trying hard to build up my clientele so I could earn enough money to get us through the summer. It was becoming harder and harder to keep up with the bills now that I had the added expenses of car insurance, gasoline and vehicle maintenance. I managed to keep the major bills paid such as rent and electricity but we often had to go without the smaller, yet basic, necessities. I wasn't able to buy things like diapers, household cleaning supplies and even toilet paper. The kids were growing like weeds and needed new clothes but I couldn't afford to buy them any. They also needed haircuts, so I decided to try to cut their hair myself. Unfortunately, that venture turned out to be a mess. Thank goodness, they weren't old enough to be worried about their appearance. They probably would have hated me.

I really wanted to be closer to God and I prayed about our problems all the time. It seemed as though the more I prayed, the worse our situation became. Whenever I grew discouraged, Salora told me that when she was in Heaven waiting to be born, Jesus told her that I was going to be her mommy. She told me that Jesus loved me. Hearing that gave me strength to continue praying and to trust that there was a reason for what we were going through. God had a plan for us.

The kids and I attended church for a while but the kid's clothes and shoes were almost threadbare and too small and I had only one decent outfit. After wearing the same clothes for three Sundays in a row, I was too embarrassed to go back so the kids and I worshipped together at home. There was never any money left over to do fun activities with the kids, which made me feel like a bad parent. When the weather was nice, we would walk to a nearby park so the kids could enjoy the playground equipment but I yearned to take them to the movies or out to dinner. Even renting a movie would have been a treat. We didn't have much but we had a television and a DVD player. However even though we stopped going to church, our ward checked on us constantly and sometimes helped provide the little things like toilet paper or clothes. It was hard for me to accept the help. But their persistence in loving us unconditionally also planted a seed that I was lovable. But at the time, it felt uncomfortable but at the same time I liked being checked on. It felt good.

I had not seen Todd other than in passing since the day we had sex so I was surprised to receive an email from him at the spa one day in early May. The message simply stated that he was sending me a client the next day, a man named Fred and that he would be paying for Fred to receive a full body massage.

Fred arrived late the next afternoon. I gave him the customary paperwork to fill out and instructed him about how to prepare himself for the massage. While he got undressed, I went to the back of the shop to take care of some things. When I re-entered the massage room, Fred was standing next to the table completely naked. I asked him to lie face down on the table and cover himself with a sheet. I left the room again. I came back after a few minutes and got a bottle of massage lotion from a shelf. Fred was dead quiet and I could tell he was not happy about something. I massaged his back first, then the backs of his legs. As I worked on his feet, he sighed, sounding bored. I could tell he was restless. Suddenly he sat up on the table and asked me if this was all he was going to get. I told him that Todd had scheduled him for a full body massage and that is what he was getting. I had no idea at that time that the term "full body massage" could be interpreted in two very different ways.

He shot me a look. A look that let me know, in no uncertain terms, that he was out of patience with me. Then he asked if we could just get on with the sex, as matter-of-factly as if he were asking for a glass of water. I was shocked and told him that I had no idea what he was talking about. Fred became enraged then and started calling me foul, filthy names. He accused me of playing silly games with him. He said he didn't want to waste time with a massage. He asked if I would perform oral sex on him. He said that he worked with Todd and that Todd had promised

50

him that I would take care of his needs. He was angry with Todd for the misunderstanding but he was even angrier with me. He thought I was just trying to act cute and coy.

I kept a cool head even though I was a little scared and talked calmly to him. I tried to get him to pay for the massage because I didn't think Todd would since I didn't deliver what he seemingly promised Fred. Fred refused, saying that Todd would give me what I deserved for the services I rendered. Needless to say he left angry and upset.

By that time, I was just glad to see him leave. When I looked at his paperwork, I saw that he had filled all of it out incorrectly. The information he supplied was all false. Evidently, he didn't want to leave a paper trail. Instead of putting the papers in a file, I tore them into little pieces and threw them in the trashcan.

The next day, when I got to the spa, one of the girls handed me an envelope. It was from Todd. To my surprise, it contained the pay for Fred's massage, one hundred dollars. I was sure Fred would have told Todd I did not deserve to be paid because I hadn't delivered what he was promised. Todd must have put it in the drop box or gave it to one of the other girls before I arrived.

I think the girls thought that the envelope contained a love note because they teased me about it. I laughed that off but I didn't try too hard to dissuade them from their notions. I couldn't risk their finding out what was actually in the envelope. I certainly couldn't explain why Todd Palin would be giving me that much money.

That money helped our situation a little but we were still struggling. One day, a couple who lived nearby asked if I would baby-sit their children while they went out for the evening. I accepted the job eagerly since every dollar I earned helped. I kept their kids at my apartment. I didn't know it at the time but taking that babysitting job led to the cementing of a relationship that continues to this day.

I was making spaghetti for our dinner and I couldn't get the lid off the jar containing the sauce. I tried all the tricks I knew. I ran warm water on it, tapped it against the edge of the table, used a dishcloth to get a better grip on the jar and pried on it with a can opener. Nothing worked so I decided to ask the man who lived in the apartment across the hall.

With four tots in tow, I knocked on his door, sauce jar in hand.

Richard was always friendly when we happened to run into each other so I didn't think he would mind lending a hand. He invited all of us in while he tried to loosen the lid. It was on so tight that even he had trouble but finally he accomplished the task, saving the day and my sanity. Dealing with four hungry children was wearing on my nerves. The next evening when I cooked dinner, I made Richard a plate, complete with chocolate chip cookies and took it to him as my way of saying thanks for the help. After that, he started dropping by to say hello to the kids and me. On nice evenings, after the kids were in bed, we sometimes sat outside on the steps and talked. Soon he asked me for a date and I accepted. We had a good time and I felt better about myself than I had in a long time. I really liked Richard and enjoyed his companionship. About two weeks after the incident with Fred and a few days after my date with Richard, Todd came into the spa. It was nearly closing time and the hairdressers had already left. Todd asked for a massage and sex. I wanted to refuse because of the feelings I had for Richard but couldn't I needed the money and, after all, I had done it with Todd already. This was going to be the last time, I told myself. Just this one last time.

I may have even had a flash of resentment toward Richard because my budding relationship was never going to be a solution to money issues. Richard was a generation older than I was but when it came to relationships, he wasn't old-fashioned about a woman working. In fact, he did not believe in men financially supporting the women with whom they were involved. He said it only complicated things and I guess he was right but having help would have made life much easier for me.

So once again, I had sex with Todd and as before, he pocketed all traces of our encounter. After we were both dressed again, I decided to confront Todd about Fred. I asked him why he hadn't told me what Fred would expect. Todd said that he thought I understood what a "full body massage," meant. I told him I did understand what the term meant and recited the description I learned during my massage therapy training. A full body massage means that the therapist will massage the whole body during a therapeutic massage. This includes the neck, shoulders, back, arms, legs, feet and hands. Upon request it may also include the abdominal area and for men, the chest. Most of the massages given at spas are full body massages.

Todd laughed, a little condescendingly. He apologized for the misunderstanding. He said that it was entirely his fault but I could tell that he thought I was dumb. He told me I had to grow up and stop acting like a little girl if I wanted to make the kind of money I needed to give my children a better life. He said that I was a great person, a woman who deserved to have a wonderful future and he just wanted to help me achieve it.

Todd told me he would send me more clients and pay me extra to cater to their whims. He said they were important people who needed someone who would understand their needs and not judge them. It went without saying that I was expected to keep quiet about their visits to me.

He promised me that I never had to have sex with anyone but said I would at least have to offer a hand job if I wanted to make extra money. He made it plain that it would be even more lucrative for me if I would provide other services. He even suggested that I advertise as Bonnie's Spa on Craigslist in the beauty category and said that I should run an Internet special. He said that he would refer people to me through the ad.

Todd did not pay me two hundred dollars for having sex with him that time. He only paid seventy-five, which was the usual price of just the massage by itself. He did not even offer me a tip. When I questioned him about the amount, he said that was all the cash he had on him but he would make it up to me later. Of course, just as it had been with the payment for that breakfast at Bee's Bakery, later never came.

I know I was crazy to let Todd keep using me the way he did but I had convinced myself that my association with him would lead to all of his wealthy friends becoming customers of mine. He always talked about sending people to me and I was gullible enough to believe him. I told him that I didn't want anymore sex clients, only regular clients. He told me if I wanted to make the kind of money I needed to give Salora and Brice a better life I had to realize that sex was what men expected. He said that if they just wanted a massage they usually went to a male masseuse. However, he promised not to refer anyone to me if that was the way I wanted it.

Looking back, I think Todd only paid me the price of the massage that time for two reasons. The first was so he could soothe his conscious by rationalizing that he hadn't paid me for sex again and the second was to help make sure that I did not get ahead of my money problems. As long as I continued to struggle financially, it was much easier for him to manipulate me into doing the things he wanted me to do.

By June, school was out and I quickly realized that my income from the spa was not going to be enough. The gambling parties that I sometimes worked at went on hiatus during the summer months because most of the regular participants were busy with hunting and fishing. I got a few jobs repairing computers, which I was skilled at but I needed something steady that I could depend on so I emailed Todd and told him he could send me some business if his offer was still good.

Most of the clients Todd sent to me were older men. Pushy, entitled and aggressive men who thought they treated me well when they really did not. They behaved crudely and thought I liked it. I don't know where they got that idea.

I gave topless massages, let them rub their penises between my breasts and gave hand jobs but I avoided actual sexual intercourse with them because I was dating Richard. They paid full prices for the services they received but rarely left a tip. Todd usually gave me an additional three hundred dollars each month but it still was not enough to make much of a difference. Something always came along and ate up any money I managed to squirrel away. Karma, I guess.

Then new money problems sprouted up. My tax refund check, which I was counting on, was held because I had defaulted on my student loan repayments. I no longer qualified for some of the assistance I had been receiving because I reported all of the income from giving massages, even the sexual ones. My kids' disability checks were discontinued because they were no longer considered disabled enough. It seemed like for every step I took forward financially, I wound up two steps back.

I began speaking to my parents again during that summer. I also agreed to let them have supervised visits with the kids. My family really was very important to me and I wanted to make every effort to repair our relationship. My parents told me that with all the financial problems I was having that the children would be better off if I gave them away and at times, I wondered if they were not right about that. Still, deep in my heart, I knew the kids belonged with me and my parents' opinion on that subject made me wonder if I would ever be able to have a good relationship with them again. How could they suggest that I give my children away?

The breaking point came one day near the end of the summer. I was having a particularly heavy period and had no sanitary pads so I had to resort to using old tee shirts that I cut into strips and folded. To top it all off, Salora was sick and I did not even have a measly buck and a half to pay the co-payment for her medicine. I decided then and there that something had to change. My children and I were not going to live this way any longer. I started seeing clients for Todd several times a week. The first time I was able to go to the grocery store and buy everything we needed, I felt incredible. I was on top of the world when I took Salora and Brice shopping for new clothes.

Anytime I felt ashamed of the way I was earning my money, I heard my parents' voices in my head, telling me that I should give the kids up for adoption and I did what I had to do to keep our family together. I kept my sanity while satisfying my client's sexual requests, some of them very strange, by reminding myself of the reasons I was doing what I did.

Some of the men wanted to have anal sex with me; some wanted me to perform anal sex on them, either with my fingers or using sex toys. Even Todd had a weird fetish. He would sometimes ask if he could have the panties I wore or ask me to rub a tissue through my vagina and he would take which ever I gave him with him when he left. Todd was running ads for me and he supplied me with a cell phone to receive his special calls. He also came up with a way for us to talk in chat rooms, message boards and special websites where people advertised for sex.

He was always thinking up new methods for us to communicate but was careful not to risk his reputation or hurt his family. Todd educated me about alternative sexual life styles and I realized how sheltered my upbringing had been. I learned the code words that were used for arranging sexual hookups for money. It was eye opening and even though I was participating in the business, I was disgusted by it.

Todd kept me motivated to continue by reminding me of what my children needed and telling me, what I wanted to hear. He told me that as his fortune grew, so would mine. He told me that one day I would be able to buy my own spa, if that was what I wanted. I did not hold much faith in that but I was glad to be able to get the things the kids and I needed.

One evening, as summer was transitioning into fall, I stayed late to give Todd a massage and of course, have sex with him. After we finished, while Todd was dressing, I went to the front of the salon to see who all was there.

I noticed Levi Johnston waiting to get a haircut. Levi probably didn't remember me but his parents might have. I lived for a short time in their neighborhood and we had seen each other out and about. Although, I don't really enjoy socializing I am a sociable person so I was always friendly whenever we saw each other.

Todd came out of the massage area and when he saw Levi, he left through the back door. Levi got up and followed Todd. I moved closer to the back and I could hear them loudly exchanging harsh words. I couldn't hear exactly what was being said but there was no doubt that they were arguing.

Levi re-entered the shop and Todd tore out of the parking lot in his truck. The sound of him squalling the tires caused people in other buildings to go outside to see what was happening. I looked at Levi and he turned away. When I realized that he and Todd must have been talking about me, I was embarrassed. I had no idea what he might say to the hairdresser.

I mention this incident here because many people

have wondered why Bristol Palin and Levi Johnston named their son Tripp. Was it a coincidence or was the boy named after me for some reason? I have my own opinion but I don't know for sure. I do know if there is a connection to my name, it would be because of what happened that day or because Todd suggested the name. Some people wonder if Levi was ever a client of mine. The answer is no.

To bring this subject to a close, the boy's name is his name and I hope people will not be negative towards him because of it. Adult issues do not need to be projected on him. I experienced this problem when I named my son but his name just fit and he grew into it. I hope that is the case with young Tripp.

In the meantime I had no idea how much Todd was really making by sending those men to me. If I had known, I would have realized how small a percentage of the money that changed hands I was receiving. I was just grateful for what money I got and that I was able to better provide for Salora and Brice. I guess what they say really is true. Ignorance is bliss.

Breathe

Upstairs that door released
      your emptiness into my sorrow's
      window beside the shore
remembered as love
left on the porch
the suitcase lonely

I just watched his eyes
empty

I felt the sunset end
I walked on the shore
moonless

clutching the sand
noticing the waves
silky and dark.

©Shailey Lawes

Chapter Four

Fall 2007

Alaska's brief summer was over all too soon. School started and I resumed subbing. I was also working at two spas, repairing computers whenever the opportunity arose and working at the gambling parties again on the weekends. All of this was in addition to seeing clients sent by Todd. Plagued by continuing money problems, I rationalized that my work for Todd was not a choice but a necessity.

The van had died. The vehicle I bought to replace it wasn't much better, and every cent left over after taking care of our basic needs went into a fund to buy our next car. As a temporary solution Richard let me have his old '88 Toyota. It was a nice gesture but it literally had pieces falling off of it every time I drove it.

By November, Todd was running "our business" like a pro. (Later on, I learned he was receiving help with it but at the time I didn't know about that.) Disposable cell phones were usually in use about two weeks when he would throw them away and hand me a new one. Legitimate-sounding advertisements for my services began to run. As far as I know they were exclusively run on the Internet on Craigslist. Some I paid for and ran, others I did not know about until much later in the future after I had been arrested. These ads contained code words that conveyed their sexual meaning to those who were looking for the services I provided. Most of the clients, several each week, came to the spas where I worked, but occasionally he had me make visits to clients' homes. After a time, Todd expanded our clientele to include women.

The sex between Todd and me continued. In fact, he expanded on that, too. He still wanted intercourse, but he also began asking me to allow him to perform oral sex on me. I despised having him do that to me. It made me feel slimy and dirty. He never asked me if I liked it, but he thought I did. His ego was enormous; he believed everything he did was wonderful. I never told him how I really felt.

He also decided that his massages and other services should be free so he stopped paying me for our encounters. I could tell that he thought I had feelings for him and that I was flattered by his attention. Nothing could have been further from the truth. I disliked him intensely and wished with all my heart that my financial situation would improve so that I could end our relationship.

Many, if not most, of the clients that Todd referred to me were as egotistical as he was. Some were even worse. Perhaps they felt elite because they were connected to the "First Dude" (the folksy title Alaskan's used when referring to the female governor's spouse). It is hard to guess what they were feeling or why. What I do know for certain is they all wore an air of superiority and no matter what subject I raised to make conversation with them, they were the supreme experts. Some tried to use their superior knowledge to educate me. I found them to be obnoxious.

Most of the men Todd sent in behaved as though they were doing me a huge favor by allowing me to attend to their needs. They requested extra services without paying anything extra. Rarely did they tip. Their attitudes made it clear that they considered me beneath them and good for only one thing. There were a few who would walk in and act like we were friends, asking me how my day had been or some other trivial personal questions. However, their attitudes became anything but friendly once servicing began. They made it clear that it was all about them and what they wanted.

Some of them came to see me after working out, and I complained that they smelled awful. They laughed at me. There were endless ways for them to show how much they disrespected me. These men wanted my sympathy,

63

though, and they'd unload their problems on me. I heard about marital problems and gambling debts. They shared their business woes and other things that were none of my concern. And in the end, they always had an excuse for why they needed my services. I didn't want to hear it. I had enough worries of my own but I had no choice but to listen. In time I found out that a lot of the stories were nothing but lies, told to me in hopes of getting a little extra attention- just another way to use me.

The policemen and lawyers connected to Todd were usually among the rudest. Some of the nicest were affiliated with B.P. British Petroleum is one of Alaska's biggest employers, and I knew those men were making good money. They could afford to pay for my services and they could have afforded a nice tip, too. There was no nice, however, when it came to getting what they wanted. If I didn't want to provide a particular service I was called names, pushed and spit on. Sometimes they threatened to report what I was doing to law enforcement. They had no consideration for my feelings or me. No one cared that I did this only as a means to support my children.

The very worst of them were the ones who became regulars. The old saying that familiarity breeds contempt was especially true when applied to my situation. After a few visits, the "regulars" would try to get out of paying me. They would claim had they already paid or leave an envelope, which, later, I would open up, and find only five dollars. I learned to stand up for myself; to be polite but stern. Money had to be paid up front and fully counted. There was no room for softness in the business. Everything about prostitution is tough.

By December, I was physically and mentally exhausted. I temporarily stopped doing the gambling parties so that I could spend more time with Salora and Brice during the holidays. I wanted my kids to have a nice Christmas and, in that respect, we were very blessed. A church adopted our family and provided us with lots of wonderful surprises. I shed many tears that Christmas. It was the first time I was actually able to cry since leaving Jimmy. I needed that emotional release; I'd forgotten how good it felt. I also started to face my honest feelings about what I was doing. Until then, I had been able to bury my guilt beneath all my rationalizations. Slowly, the truth seeped into my consciousness.

The New Year brought more changes and a lot of emotional pain. Richard and I had survived a rocky period between Thanksgiving and Christmas, and I was clinging to the fact that he loved me and the kids. I told myself we could work through our issues and by Christmas it seemed like we had.

Then, Richard decided he was moving to Anchorage. When he told me this, he led me to believe the kids and I were going with him—that we would get a place together. He even got newspapers and apartment guides so he and I could search together for our new home. I was so excited. Finally, I would get away from Todd Palin. No longer would I have to prostitute myself to support my family. My trust in Richard was complete. My guard was down. I should have known better.

One day I came home early and the apartment building manger stopped me and asked me to verify the date when Richard was moving out. I felt confused, lost, like I had missed part of a conversation. I just stood there. He asked me again, he said he needed to schedule a walk through. I told him I would tell Richard and check on the move out date. By this point I was fuming, angry and disgusted with myself. I felt like such an idiot. A fool. I wondered how he could do this to me, not to mention my kids who had bonded with him. Why bother pretending he wanted to look at apartments with me? We even had a showing scheduled! He had never said a word about having already found a new place.

When I confronted him it led us to having a huge fight. Fighting with Richard was so different than fighting with anyone else I had been with before. It was mostly me telling him off and calling him foul names. He was very quiet. All he said was yes, you are right. I was used to back and forth drama ending with someone giving in. Richard never gave in. He just moved. He said he would keep in touch with the kids and would just accept that he and I would not be speaking very much. He got very involved in his life in Anchorage. I continued to be hurt. I sulked and wallowed in my feelings of betrayal.

My breakup with Richard and his leaving were emotionally devastating. Soon enough, though, something happened to take my mind off Richard. Jimmy wanted custody of the kids!

It's a messed up world when a man who attempted to kill his wife and children is not only free to walk the streets but free to file for custody of the children whose lives he tried to end. The authorities in Alabama considered arresting Jimmy a waste of time. They didn't think I would cooperate by returning from Alaska to testify against him if and when the case ever went to trial. Furthermore, the police felt strongly that if the kids and I did come back Jimmy would kill all of us so they actively discouraged our return.

Jimmy didn't really want custody, of course. He wanted to hurt me and used the kids to do so. He had obtained a default divorce from me in Alabama. Unfortunately, it wasn't legal because I received no notification to which I could respond. There was a court proceeding in Alaska in which they found him to have fraudulently filed for his divorce in Alabama. I wanted a divorce with a clear, unquestionable custody order, but I couldn't afford an attorney. Jimmy didn't get custody, but unfortunately I didn't get the divorce, either. I did get a clear child support order and to date he is in arrears of sixty thousand dollars. Through all my trials and issues with their father, in front of the children I only spoke considerately about Jimmy, and continue to do so. It isn't easy. Especially because I try my best to never lie to my kids, so when they ask about him or want to look at pictures of him it is hard. He disgusts me, but because of their desire to know about him, I hide my feelings as best as I can and do what I have to do.

By mid-January of 2008, I was literally running myself ragged. My car had conked out completely and I needed another one as soon as possible so I could get to all my jobs, so I resumed subbing at the schools and I took another massage therapist position Monday through Friday, with a local chiropractor. Dr. Morgan had offices in both Wasilla and Anchorage.

Since I was getting paid per massage he was willing to schedule the clients around my other jobs. Weekday evenings I gave massages at Bonnie's or filled in at another spa in Wasilla. Six clients for Todd came to see me at Bonnie's and he deposited $350.00 dollars into my bank account that month. A computer job would come along about once a week, and I still worked at gambling parties. Anything I could do to make a few extra bucks, I did. My time with the kids was down to about one hour a day during the week. I felt like a terrible parent for not spending more time with them but I thought providing for them financially was the most important thing. I now know that children thrive on attention and material things aren't nearly as important in the long term. Basic physical needs must be met, of course. It was a good feeling when I could buy diapers, clothes and food for my growing children. I wanted to be free from worrying about where I was going to get the money to pay the bills. I felt a sense of pride too when I could buy other things for my children. Purchasing a simple thing like a new towel was a thrill to me.

On Saturdays, I started taking college classes,

hoping to improve myself so I could be a better provider for Salora and Brice. Since I had defaulted on my student loans, I wasn't eligible for assistance. I paid for my classes and I paid my parents to watch Salora and Brice while I went to school because they continued to resist being a help to me. My friends and family told me I was crazy to add to my financial burden by going back to school but I thought if I could get my degree it would help my situation in the long run. Besides that, I thought I deserved to do something for myself. Going back to school was a miracle for me, emotionally, and I made the Dean's list every semester while enrolled. (I still lack seven classes to graduate but I have made a resolution that I will finish one day.)

February was a hard month. Salora and Brice both had birthdays. Salora's is early in the month and Brice's near the end. I wanted to do something special, separately, for both of them but with my limited funds, the best I could manage was a trip to McDonald's mid-way through the month, combining the celebration of their special days. The kids were happy but I felt like a failure. The mom in me wished she could have hosted parties for both of them and given them lots of presents.

Salora continued having seizures and began complaining that her eyes hurt. I wrote a note so I wouldn't forget to mention it at her next doctor appointment. The hospital that had examined Salora's arm called to schedule her surgery for May, giving me the added worry of an expensive trip to Seattle. I knew there was no use in asking my parents. And I wouldn't have asked Richard even if we had been on better terms because I knew how he felt about lending money. I had no emotional support, no financial support, and no good solutions. It's no wonder I became depressed and stopped socializing with my friends. What little free time I had, I spent with the children.

Todd sent me nine clients that February - three more than the previous month; and yet the deposit he made into my account was same amount as in January. Not one penny more, even though I saw half-again as many people as before, plus Todd visited me himself once during the month. Todd was taking advantage of me and exploiting me.

I was a robot. I was programmed to do whatever I was told. I never asked questions. I accepted and was grateful for whatever Todd paid me.

Two good things happened in February. I finally got a decent car and joining Dr. Morgan's office was working out really well. Dr. Morgan knew I needed more income, and he recommended me to a woman running a women's health clinic in Anchorage, helping make arrangements for me to provide massage services on a part-time basis at their health spa.

The first week in March, I was at the women's clinic picking up my check and Lorraine, the owner, asked if I would mind giving some woman a massage. The client was a VIP, she said, and her regular therapist wasn't working. It meant extra money, so I was glad to do it. Lorraine told me which room the woman was in and I hurried down the hall with no idea of the shock I was about to receive. I knocked lightly on the door before I opened it and entered. When I saw who was in the room I wanted to go through the floor or disappear in a cloud of smoke. The woman sitting on the massage table was Governor Sarah Palin!

I could feel my face flushing and I hoped that she wouldn't notice. I introduced myself, trying not to stutter. Needing a minute to compose myself, I told her that I had to get some forms so I could go over some things with her before we got started, and I hurried out of the room. If I could have, I would have run out the back door and kept on going. But, I couldn't do that because-and this must be the hundredth time I've written this-I really needed the job. My stomach churned and my mind raced with questions. What was Sarah Palin doing here? Had someone told her that something was going on between Todd and me? Was she here to confront me? What would I say if she asked me if I was having an affair with her husband?

I took a deep breath and tried to calm myself down. I went into the restroom and looked at myself in the mirror. As I expected, my face was beet red. I wet a paper towel with cold water and placed it across my forehead. I willed myself to think. I had only been working here for a couple of weeks and only a few people knew I was giving massages here. I couldn't remember whether I had mentioned it to Todd or not but he certainly wouldn't have said anything to Sarah about me. Would he?

I finally convinced myself it was just a coincidence that she was here. She was a regular client here and being the governor she would expect to receive service even if she didn't have an appointment. I washed my face with the paper towel, tossed it in the trash and smoothed my hair down. You can handle this, I told myself over and over. I exited the restroom and went to the small office where we kept patient charts and blank forms. I selected the documents that I needed and went back to the room where Sarah waited. She gave me a look that conveyed that she didn't appreciate being kept waiting for so long. I offered no apology.

I thought to myself she's just another client, she's no different than anyone else and in a businesslike tone began asking the questions that were required before beginning a massage. To the question about being on any medication, especially blood thinners, she replied that she was on some type of blood pressure medicine. She didn't say whether she was being treated for low blood pressure or high blood pressure. I informed her that some blood pressure medications can act as a blood thinner and therefore I would not use really firm pressure. That was the only drug she was taking but she told me she had recently received lipodissolve injections in her abdomen for weight

loss. We moved on through the questions, and I asked if she had any major health problems, any surgeries in the past three years and if there was any possibility that she was pregnant. She replied no to all three questions.
I then inquired if there was any special reason she wanted a massage or was it just for relaxation.

She said that it had been recommended that she get a massage because her neck was stiff and her abdominal area was sore. She also exhibited general stiffness and an inability to relax.

Sarah chose to lay face down, and I began the massage. With her lying on her stomach, I didn't have to look at her face and I could pretend I didn't know who she was. Her muscles were very tense and didn't respond well to medium pressure, so I used light pressure and kneading. Her neck and shoulders were very stiff and I noted on the forms that she might benefit from a chiropractic evaluation. When I had her roll over onto her back we could see each other; I became nervous again. If she were going to confront me now would be the time. To my relief, she showed no such intention. She was blasé. I relaxed and began massaging her shoulders. After a few minutes she requested that I massage her abdomen, explaining that the nurse had told her massage would help flush out the extra fluids from the lipodissolve injection and might help with the tenderness. I was a bit disconcerted by her request but I did as she asked and began to massage her stomach through the thin sheet. Her abdominal area was very sore and the pain wasn't relieved by the massage so I suggested ten minutes of heat therapy. When the heat therapy was finished I asked her if there was anything else I could do for her. She said no so I told her she could get dressed.

She removed the sheet and got down from the table. I was surprised that she hadn't waited for me to leave the room before uncovering as most clients did but since she was standing almost nude in front of me I couldn't help peeking surreptitiously at the woman to whom Todd was married. I compared my full figure to her slender, toned body and wondered what Todd saw in me.

I left to do the post-massage paperwork for her chart. She dressed, and when I went back in, I recommended to her that she see her doctor about the abdominal tenderness to rule out a urinary tract infection. She thanked me and left. No tip. I didn't care. I was just relieved that she was gone and one of the longest hours of my life was finally over.

The rest of the month was routine until the last week when Todd came to me for sex. When I told him about my encounter with Sarah and how worried I had been, he laughed. I really wanted to slap him. Once again, he didn't pay me. He didn't have to say it, I knew he felt entitled to freebies since he sent clients to me and I was paid for the services I gave them. I wanted to tell him to stop sending clients to me and never show his face to me again. I really, really wanted to. Salora's surgery was coming up though, so I kept my mouth shut.

April was a busy month. My job with the chiropractor didn't pay all that well and it was eating up time. Added to the massages I was doing at the women's clinic and making time for Salora and Brice, I knew something had to give. I decided to stop doing the gambling parties. I had already notified the school system at the end of March that I was no longer available to be a substitute. I enjoyed working at the schools but it was interfering with my schedule now that I was working at the women's clinic and the massage jobs paid better than subbing.

Around mid- April, Dr. Morgan and Lorraine had a falling out. She said she'd still like me to work for her so she contracted with me directly. This meant I was still working three jobs; offering massages at Dr. Morgan's office, Bonnie's spa, and Lorraine's women's clinic. Four, counting the business I handled for Todd. I was tired but grateful for all of the work because it helped me save up for the upcoming trip to Seattle and the period of time I wouldn't be earning anything because I would be at the hospital with Salora.

One day I was scheduled to give several massages at the clinic. A few of the other girls and I were eating lunch in the employees' lounge and watching television. The mid-day news came on and the big story was that Governor Sarah Palin had given birth earlier that morning to a baby boy.

All our jaws dropped simultaneously. All of us had seen her here at one time or another over the past few months. It had only been about six weeks since the day I had given her the massage and she hadn't looked the least bit pregnant. I had massaged her abdomen and saw her in the nude. I hadn't noticed anything to make me think she was pregnant much less only a few weeks away from giving birth. I also distinctly remembered asking her if she was pregnant and her saying no.

I heard the news reporter say that the baby was premature and would face special challenges. I felt a bit of sympathy for Sarah when I heard that. I knew all too well what it was like to raise children with special needs. I assumed that the baby being premature explained why neither I nor any of the other staff had noticed that she was pregnant.

I went to the office, pulled Sarah's chart and brought it back to the lounge. The other girls and I looked at it. Just as I thought, she had denied being pregnant. Reading over her chart, all of us were appalled at some of the procedures she had undergone while pregnant.
One of the girls began to cry. Was there a possibility that the treatments Sarah had received here might have caused the baby's problems? I told her that she had no reason to feel guilty. I told her that Sarah probably hadn't realized

she was pregnant.

If I had known at that time that Sarah and Todd's son was only one month premature and weighed over six pounds, I would have wondered how in the world Sarah could not have known she was expecting. I would also have wondered where the fetus was hiding when I massaged her abdomen because I hadn't seen or felt anything that indicated that she was pregnant.

Later, I would learn much more about the many strange occurrences surrounding the birth of Todd and Sarah's youngest child. However, at that time I had so much going on in my own life that I just said a prayer for the baby and put any thoughts that something was odd about his mother's pregnancy and the child's birth out of my head.

I saw eight people that Todd referred in April. Most of them came to see me at Bonnie's but a couple of them showed up at the clinic even though I specifically asked Todd not to send anyone there. The two men he sent to the clinic were important people and I believe Todd thought that the spa at the clinic would make a better impression on them because it was more upscale. Once again he paid me $350.00 dollars.

I knew I should be getting more and I started to ask Todd why he wasn't paying me according to the number of clients he sent but I chickened out. Todd had a short fuse and his mood could change in a minute. He had grabbed my arm more than once in anger so I tried to avoid doing anything that might set his temper off.

May arrived and I informed Todd that I would be away for a few days, possibly more, in the middle of the month. I hadn't planned on telling him where I was going or why but he kept pushing me for answers, so eventually I told him that Salora was having surgery in Seattle. Later on, I wished I hadn't told him where I was going because he used the information to arrange more work for me. It was a somewhat different type of work, but no better. Maybe even worse and I wasn't comfortable doing it.

Even so, Todd wasn't happy that I was going to be unavailable for a while. He told me that I needed to pay for the ads myself and supply my own cell phones. I thought it was because he was angry at me but he said it was to build my reputation so people would recognize my name when I opened my own spa. If I had been thinking straight I would have realized that was baloney. How would running ads for massage therapy services that contained code words for sexual acts help me get a good reputation when I opened a legitimate spa? But my mind was on Salora's upcoming surgery and being separated from Brice. I did as Todd instructed without giving it much thought. With the benefit of hindsight I realize that having me pay for everything protected Todd. He could refer people to me without having it traced back to him. If I got arrested for prostitution, he wouldn't be discovered through cell phones or ads.

Todd couldn't afford to have his reputation tarnished. He made sure that he was protected even if it meant throwing me to the wolves. A few days before I had to take Salora to Seattle, Richard called me. He said that he knew Salora's surgery was coming up and offered to stay with Brice while I was gone. I accepted gratefully because that saved me from having to pay my parents to keep him. However, a local church then offered to help not only with the cost of the trip to Seattle but to also care for Brice while I was gone. I felt that was a better arrangement because I didn't want Brice becoming too attached to Richard again since we were no longer romantically involved. However, Richard did come to visit us everyday when Salora and I returned home and he spent a little extra time with Brice. It was wonderful having him back in my life and it made me realize how much I had missed him.

Salora's operation was successful to a degree, but

she would still need more surgery down the road. I was just glad to have that one behind us and be back at home.

The clients Todd was sending to me now were important people-business executives and high-ranking military officers-who shared one common trait. They were aggressive. These men weren't satisfied with a hand job. I should have stood my ground but I was already degraded and worn out. I didn't have the energy to argue. It was easier for me to just have sex with them.

Over that summer, Todd began acting differently. He no longer wanted to have sex with me. He rarely even requested a massage. When we met he was formal and businesslike. He was also secretive, always wanting to meet me in unfamiliar places and never the same place twice. He gave me a notebook and told me to keep records on each client. He wanted their addresses and phone numbers. He had me list the services they requested, which services were their favorites, and if they ever asked if other girls were available. Anything I thought was interesting, Todd wanted recorded.

Todd also arranged for me to meet with some women who had been "in the business" for a long time. They gave me some tips about how to handle clients when they got rowdy and what to say to the clients when they wanted me to do something that I wasn't willing to do. One of the women was a lot like me, or, I should say, used to be a lot like me. She was a single mother who had struggled with financial hardships and had worked more than one job simultaneously.

Now she was a glamorous woman working for a company in Seattle in a position with the job title Entertainment Public Relations representative. Her only duties were to take the clients, who were mostly from other countries, out on the town and show them a good time. That sounded good to me. I thought I'd like a position similar to hers.

Summer was peaceful for the most part. I saw very few clients for Todd, and there were no gambling parties to work. But I was able to keep the bills paid through my regular massage jobs and repairing a few computers here and there.

At the end of August, I learned the reason I hadn't seen Todd very much over the last couple of months. Politics, never on my radar, was suddenly the only topic in town, or more accurately, in the entire state. All of Alaska was abuzz with the news that Sarah Palin had been chosen by Republican Presidential candidate John McCain as his running mate.

With the Palins in the lower forty-eight during September and October, my life, for the most part, was uneventful. Todd did pay me a visit when he came home for a few days in September. He wanted a massage and sex. As usual, he didn't pay me. I guess he thought I should be honored to screw the man that might soon be the whole country's "First Dude." Frankly, I thought dud was more like it.

Todd did keep in touch with me while he and Sarah were on the campaign trail. He set up email accounts for me so that I could receive messages from him. Every couple of weeks he would make a new email account and delete the old. He never inquired how I was doing or how the kids were or if I was making it financially. He just wanted to know if I was hearing from the people that he had referred. I didn't tell Todd this, but the cell phone associated with the number running in the ads at that time was gone. I'd thrown it in the trash. So when he asked about hearing from his people, I just said I hadn't heard from them. I wasn't lying. It may have been disingenuous, but I couldn't resist suggesting that probably they were too busy watching all the political stuff on television leading up to the big election. That seemed to flatter him and he didn't ask any more questions.

Too soon though, the elections were over and the Palins returned to Alaska. I didn't pay much attention to Sarah but Todd seemed to have his tail tucked between his legs, licking his wounds. He came to see me in December. To my surprise, he was not the dapper Todd I was used. He looked like an ordinary Alaskan in his blue jeans, plaid flannel shirt and well-worn coat. His physical appearance, unshaven, tired eyes, and pale skin, matched his attire. At first, I thought the stress of being in the limelight for months had taken a toll on him. But after spending a little time with him I realized the real reason for his depression was that he missed having national attention. Being the First Dude of Alaska was nothing but a big letdown for him now.

When we had sex, he needed constant reassurance that he was handsome and that he was a great lover. He wanted to be told how well endowed he was and that he was a man any woman would desire.

I believe I could have been rid of Todd Palin forever if I had told him at that time that he was nothing special. He would have left and never bothered me again. But me being me, I couldn't tear him down. I knew all too well, from personal experience, what that did to a person. So, instead, I offered him the reassurance he was looking for. That turned out to be a mistake, of course, and I began another two years of torture, trouble and heartache.

Remember

I open my eyes,
gaze into the hazy sky
The sun a-flare
as I smile and inhale the sweet air.
I am filled with love, warmth, and glee
a sense of wholeness within me....

©Shailey Lawes

Chapter Five

Christmas 2008

After the disappointment of the November election, Todd seemed to throw himself into running the business and was even more assertive than he had been before. I regretted that I hadn't told him what I really thought of him when I had the opportunity. He got me another phone and placed more ads, wording them so that our regular clients would recognize them as mine. I saw quite a few sexual clients just before Christmas. Todd himself came in for my services, too, and didn't pay or tip.

Only one man gave me a bonus—one hundred dollars. Strangely enough, it came from the client I despised the most. This was a man who turned my stomach with all the vile, disgusting things he paid me to do. In a way, I wanted to refuse to take his "gift." There could have been satisfaction in throwing the money back in his face. But I kept it. It wasn't really a gift. I had more than earned it.

My parents had invited the kids and me to the family Christmas get together. Salora, Brice and I were all looking forward to it. But a few days before the event, they asked us not to come. They said my brother and some of the other people who would be there were uncomfortable with the idea of the kids and me attending.

It's hard to describe how deeply hurt I was about my children and I being rejected that way. It was cruel. It hurt a lot. Nevertheless, I had to deal with it. The hardest part was telling the kids that we wouldn't be going to Grandma and Grandpa's house. I didn't want Salora and Brice to think badly of their grandparents, so I told them that Grandma was sick. They were disappointed, but they understood what it was to be sick. It was a harmless lie, I guess.

Then there was someone else who said he cared about us and wanted us to be a part of his Christmas day. Richard promised that we would be together for Christmas; no matter what. He'd invited his daughters, Brandy and Callista, too. Anticipating our holiday gathering-Richard and me, my children and Richard's grown girls-I was happy.

Richard arrived Christmas morning, as expected. But almost immediately, he said he could only stay for a short time. He said he had to go back to his apartment in Anchorage and get ready to go see his daughters. The children and I were not invited after all. Why? What happened to our plans? I wanted to know. I *needed* to know.

Richard said it wouldn't be appropriate for us to be there because Michelle (his ex wife), Brandy and Callista's mother, would be there as well. This upset me terribly. Richard knew how hurt I already was because my parents didn't want the kids and me at their holiday celebration and then he compounded that hurt by breaking his promise that we would spend the holiday together. I argued that the way he was treating the children and me wasn't appropriate, either. Richard didn't stay quiet this time. He argued. We began hurling insults at one another, and it became a huge argument.

Absolutely livid, I gave him an ultimatum. If he went to spend Christmas with his daughters and ex-wife without the kids and me, we were finished. He walked out the door. Salora and Brice asked why Mr. Rich couldn't stay with us. I told them he had to leave because Brandy and Callista would be sad if he didn't come to see them on Christmas Day. They began crying. They kept asking why we couldn't go with him. My kids were as brokenhearted as I was.

It took a while before the lure of the toys that Santa had left claimed their attention and eased their disappointment. It was a lot harder for me to get over Richard's treatment of us. I spent a lot of time just sitting and thinking, trying to remember if I had done something to deserve this.

Richard and Michelle had been separated for a couple of years when he and I met. And when I found out that he hadn't filed for a divorce, I told him he had to if we were going to continue our relationship. He did, and their divorce had been finalized for only a few weeks. Now Richard, Michelle, and their daughters were all gathering for Christmas like a happy family and the kids and I were treated like outcasts.

It made no sense. I would have understood if Brandy and Callista had been children, but these were grown women in their twenties. Surely, something could have been arranged so that we could all celebrate together. But, instead, everyone had rejected us. Christmas afternoon, some members of our church family dropped by with gifts and food and stayed for a couple of hours. I was glad to see them and I tried to enjoy their company, but I'm sure they could tell I was upset about something. Truthfully, I was relieved when they left because it was difficult to pretend that I was having a wonderful day.

Over the next couple of days Salora, Brice, and I stayed at home and did Christmas - related stuff together. We had been invited to activities at several of the local churches and Family Promise but I was so upset that neither Richard nor my family thought we were worth spending time with during the holidays that I didn't want to go anywhere. Finally, after two days of sitting home feeling sorry for myself, I packed the kids up and took them over to my parents' house. The children enjoyed it. They received more gifts and it was like a mini - Christmas for them. Thank goodness they were too young to notice the tension between the other adults and me. This was also a time in which I was really grateful for the church and the ward and the wonderful and selfless attention they gave to us. It is just I was craving that from my parents and getting no where. So instead of appreciating what I did have at that time I wanted the same attention from people who for their own reasons and hurt, were not able to give it to me or my children.

The last few days of December were uneventful. I worked for Dr. Morgan and Lorraine. I was still renting space at Bonnie's and saw a few legitimate clients there. I didn't see any sexual clients, and, in fact, I hadn't heard from Todd in over a week. I was glad about that. With everything I was going through with Richard and my parents, the last thing I needed to deal with was Todd Palin and his demanding clients.

The children kept asking where Mr. Rich was so I told them that he was really busy and we might not see him for a long time. They didn't say much after that, but I could tell they missed him. Richard had become like a father to them. I missed him too but his rejection on Christmas day had me wondering if he was ready for another relationship or if he was still in love with his ex-wife. As the clock struck midnight on New Year's Eve, I sat by myself watching a celebration on television and I wondered if I was destined to always be alone. Every man who I thought loved me had let me down. Was I that unlovable? Had I been born with some flaw that repelled men? I didn't know the answers.

In utter despair, my heart ached, my soul felt sick. That night I slept very little. When I woke up I knew I needed to change. From that moment on I prayed every day, whenever the time felt right. Some days I prayed silent prayers all day long-please God help me change my life, let me be able to care for my children. And please, God, help me with my temper. Help me be patient. Please help me wake up and have the energy to go to school. Praying became so ingrained into my lifestyle I even saw my kids start to do it. It wasn't a conscious act, but this act of prayer and releasing the pain in little pieces throughout the day helped immensely.

In January, I started my next semester at college. I was going to classes several nights a week and on Saturdays. I loved school even though it was taking a toll on me and on my budget. Continuing my education meant more than covering the cost of classes. It also meant paying for childcare and filling the car's gas tank more often. About the time my tuition was due for the spring semester, Todd asked me to start seeing clients again. Working for Todd now was very different than it had been before Sarah's candidacy for Vice-President. He told me that we had to be very careful because the Palins were famous now. He stressed over and over again that if I messed up and we got caught it would be him and his family who would suffer the most. He developed a special method for us to communicate with each other to minimize his risk.

Todd would leave a one-word note on the windshield of my car or make a chalk mark on my tire. These were signals to put me on notice to expect a phone call or email from him soon with instructions. Todd usually made the calls from other people's phones and emailed from free accounts he set up with false information. He didn't want anything to be traced back to him. Sometimes, though, he would slip up and email from his .gov or B.P. email accounts. Once I got the phone call or email, I would know where I was meeting the client and would make arrangements for someone to stay with Salora and Brice so I could go back to "work."

I must admit that I kind of liked the cloak and dagger feel of the way we were doing things. It gave me an adrenaline rush at times. An odd thing was that when Todd was the client he always wanted to be seen at Bonnie's. I told him we were taking a risk by doing it there but he always insisted. Sure enough, we were caught a couple of times by the cleaning women, Donna and Sheryl. Bonnie even came in once while Todd and I were there, causing me to turn as red as a pickled beet. Fortunately for Todd, Donna and Sheryl knew how to keep a secret. As for Bonnie, she just looked the other way, so to speak, since she was a friend of Todd's. Todd had a lot of women friends.

Another aspect of Todd trying to be extra careful, was that he was only referring clients that he already knew. That man I despised who gave me the Christmas bonus? He was making appointments with me regularly. He really made me sick. He was an executive with GCI (the communications company) and he was so full of himself. He talked to no end about all the charities he donated money to and all the wonderful things he did for people. Believe me, his treatment of me was anything but wonderful.

The services he requested were vile and repulsive. He obviously thought he was God's gift to women and thought there was nothing wrong with the things he wanted from me. He said that if he was going to pay me he was going to get what he paid for. Many times after seeing this particular client, I told myself I was going to call Todd and quit. Then I would think about bills, rent, car payments, utility costs, daycare fees, school tuition, groceries and my resolve would away. When my groceries were rung up, or the pharmacy had a prescription ready for one of my kids, I didn't care that some of the money I was handing over came from Todd Palin's referrals, it felt good.

When it came time to see clients, though, it didn't feel good, and I had to hype myself up by reminding myself of how terrible I had felt when I couldn't provide for my children. Those memories were enough to keep me going. In desperate times, people do desperate things. What I had gotten involved with is called "the oldest profession in the world." It was a tough road I had taken, but it could have been even worse. Thankfully, I never turned to drugs and alcohol even when they were offered to get me through what I was doing. I do understand why some women and men in the business become dependent on those substances. I probably would have as well had I continued for another year.

By early spring of 2009, I was serious about making some positive changes in my life. For one thing, I decided I was going to open a computer business. And also, Richard and I were getting close again we were talking about me and the kids moving in with him. (Had I followed my heart, I would have jumped on his offer, but my head told me to take a wait and see approach.)

Around the same time as Richard's offer for us to move in with him, Todd asked me to make a short trip to Fairbanks to take care of some important clients. He had suggested I go on trips before but I had always refused. This time for a number of reasons, not the least being I needed some time away from Richard to consider his offer, I agreed to go.

I would only be away for the weekend. I arranged for Richard and a friend from church to look after Salora and Brice. My mom agreed to pitch in, too, if she was needed. They all thought I was going to a computer expo event to promote my computer business. I flew out on a Friday night, I was given a nice room in a suite and the best of food was provided all weekend. The cost of the trip was put on my first client's credit card. All he wanted was a hand job and some attention. Unfortunately, others that weekend weren't so undemanding, including the nasty guy from GCI. These were important men in high positions whose behavior was revolting. There were also a couple of women there who kept trying to talk up what I call the party hostess lifestyle for lack of a better term.

They were single mothers in similar situations to mine and both of them told me that Todd was the one who brought them into the business. These women were high most of the time and said mean things to me. They let me know they saw me as fat and unattractive. Their remarks didn't really bother me; and they were upset when the men preferred to spend time with me.

It was a weird situation and I was glad when Sunday came and it was time to leave. Ironically, I met a man in the lobby of the hotel and we discussed my returning to Fairbanks later to do some security programming for his business. That lessened my guilt over lying about the reason for my trip. Todd paid me $800.00 when I got back from Fairbanks and with that money in my bank account in case things didn't work out, I decided the kids and I would move in with Richard. I thought that I would finally be in a position to end things with Todd once and for all but I soon found out that getting out of the line of work I was doing was much more difficult than getting into it.

Fury of the Sky
  Standing in the soft meadow,
    Shades of pink dance in the sky
A light breeze
  The gentle patter of rain
    The divine presence is felt with a
force,
And suddenly - A Clap
Of thunder - BOOMING
LOUD
Smooth waves of brilliant light,
  Caught fast in a timeless dream -
    Enchanted wonder
Enhancing the mind

While gazing into the fury of the sky.

©Shailey Lawes

Chapter Six

Summer 2009

Moving in with Richard in Anchorage opened up a completely new world for the kids and me. No more long car rides to the hospital and doctors' offices and we lived near the Y and could go as a family for the children's therapy. There was so much to do in the city and with my financial problems lessened, I decided to stop seeing Todd and the clients he sent.

When I told Todd, I didn't want to see him or his friends again he was flabbergasted. He agreed to leave me alone but I could tell he wasn't happy about my decision. He positioned himself very close to me, placed his hand on my arm and told me that I needed him and I would be back.

It wasn't at all romantic. It was creepy and he had this strange, almost menacing, expression on his face. I was glad that I wouldn't be seeing him anymore but worried that he might not leave me alone. Even though Richard took care of all the living expenses, I still had bills to pay so I couldn't give up my job as a massage therapist entirely.

I decided to see only my regular female clients and I would only see them at Bonnie's. I sent out postcards and emails announcing my new policy. A few of the men still came by and asked if I would make an exception just this once. It felt so good to tell them no. To my surprise, Todd didn't bother me at all

By the end of the summer, I was feeling really close to Richard and beginning to harbor hopes that he would ask me to marry him. It seemed as if my life was finally becoming what I was always hoping it would be. I was in a stable relationship with a man who cared for me and acted as a father to my kids. We were living in a nice apartment in a gated community.

I was able to cut my work hours to a minimum and was spending a lot of time with Salora and Brice. I was going to school at night and I was getting ready to open my computer business. I told Bonnie my last day at the spa would be in August. My life was as near to perfect as it had ever been.

In late July, Richard started talking to me about all of us going to Ohio to meet his family. I was so excited. It finally felt like we were a real couple and he wanted his family to know us. The plans for the trip were finalized. We were scheduled to leave just before Labor Day. The air smelled fresher. My burdens seemed lighter, and I felt very close to Richard at that moment in time. We had overcome so many problems, set backs and misunderstandings to get to this point. At last, our relationship seemed to be moving in the direction I had always wanted it to go.

My guard came all the way down. I had a feeling that Richard was going to propose while we were in Ohio. My euphoria spilled over to the kids. We started talking about all of Dad's relatives and who they were. The kids caught my happiness bug. The rest of the summer went by in a heartbeat. It was the best summer I ever had. Ever.

As August rolled in, Richard and I began making the final plans to get my computer business up and running. We both felt that obtaining office space should be our top priority. While we looked for an office, we made plans to incorporate and discussed ways to gain business. It was an exciting, busy time. One day while I was running an errand, I saw Todd.

My heart froze for a second and I felt prickles of fear on the back of my neck. Before I could look away, he saw me and signaled for me to follow him to a nearby parking lot. I didn't and the next thing I knew his vehicle was behind mine. Not wanting him following me, I pulled into a drive-thru coffee stand parking lot, hoping that he would keep going. He didn't.

He pulled in, parked next to me and rolled his window down. He motioned for me to roll mine down, too. Suddenly, he reminded me of a slick used car salesman; kind of sleazy and always trying to make a sale. I had never thought of him in that way before. He had this smile on his face that made me uncomfortable.

"How are you?" I asked not wanting him to see that he had discomfited me.

"We are having problems," he paused for a few seconds before continuing. "My kids are doing great and I can see you have been busy."

"I've had a great summer. Richard and I, our relationship is much stronger now."

"I see you now live over on 56th street." How did he know that, I wondered.

He proceeded to let me know he knew where we went for therapy and what our daily routine was in general. This unnerved me and my street-smart survival instincts kicked in. I realized he had never left my life and I knew something was going to happen. Something I would not like.

This was never going to end. I should have known he was not going to let go of me that easily. He had just been biding his time, waiting to pounce. I sighed, "Well you seem to know a lot. What do you want?"
"Let's go somewhere and talk" Todd replied.

I looked around the area where we were and told him that I knew a place where we could go. We went to one of my favorite coffee houses where we could be indoors and have a measure of privacy. It was a place where the staff knew me and wouldn't hesitate to help me if necessary.

We sat down at a table and ordered two coffees. I didn't speak. In my heart, I hoped that maybe Todd just wanted closure but in my head, I knew that my fears were confirmed. He began asking questions that were obviously posed so he could gauge where I was financially. I proudly told him that I was almost ready to open my computer business and was looking for office space. Almost as soon as the words left my mouth, I realized the mistake I had made.

I tried to back pedal and make like I was just exaggerating about my big plans but Todd didn't even seem to hear me. He started mentioning places he knew with office space available and how I might be able to use him as a reference. He quickly brought up the idea that there might be enough space to see massage clients in a back room.

When I told him that was out of the question, he reminded me that my clientele always followed me wherever I went. He also pointed out that I wouldn't even have to service the clients myself. He suggested that I find a woman to handle that aspect of the business. He said adding a massage therapy component to the business would assure its success. As he talked, wheels were turning in my head. I was worried about the computer business being successful. I didn't want it to fail because I knew my family would never let me live that down. Moreover, Todd was right about clients following me.

I also knew that Todd wasn't ever going to let me go. I figured I might as well make the best of things, as well as some money. I told Todd I would try to find someone to provide services. Once I told Todd I would go along with his plans, he quickly wrapped up our meeting. He told me he would be in touch and left, leaving me to pay for our coffees. This was typical Todd.

A couple of days later, Todd called my cell phone. He wanted me to see some clients for him at a hotel in Anchorage. He told me to tell Richard and my family that I was going to Atlanta for a computer fair. I would only need to be away for a weekend and the money he offered was good, so I agreed.

I spent that weekend in a fancy hotel. I saw several clients for Todd and saw Todd, as well. We interviewed a woman named Lanell Stanley who had emailed me in response to an online ad I placed. Lanell was a sweet, likeable person but I should have realized from the start that she was big trouble. I should have done a background check but hindsight is 20/20 and I was in a hurry to get everything finalized before the trip to Ohio. Todd thought she was perfect so I agreed.

As soon as the weekend was over, I began looking for office space. I found a suitable location and signed the lease. Things were moving quickly and in my excitement, I let my guard down. I should have known better because Todd soon took over.

He recommended renovations and made suggestions about the furnishings. The most puzzling thing he did, however, was insist that I add Lanell's name to the lease. I asked him why her name should be on the lease and that's when he told me that he wanted me to make more trips for him. Lanell's name needed to be on the lease so she could do business and take care of any problems that might come up while I was away. I could never have dreamed of all the problems that she and to a lesser extent, Todd, would cause while I was in Ohio.

ScwoochSchwooch

Schwooch Schwooch
shimmy shimmy mo -may
Schwooch Schwooch
shimmy shimmy mo-may
screeitch, screeitch, ch-ch-ch sssssmont
screeitch, screeitch, ch-ch-ch sssssmont
rolls the old boat in the lock
Schwooch Schwooch
shimmy shimmy mo-may
scraping diligently against the dock
screeitch, screeitch, ch-ch-ch sssssmont
paint falls off, chunks afloat of metal
screeitch, screeitch, ch-ch-ch sssssmont
engine trying hard to turn - puffs -
smokes - settle
Schwooch Schwooch
shimmy mo-may
my poor little boat astray.

©Shailey Tripp

Chapter Seven

Fall 2009-March2010

    All of us left for Ohio; as a family. I was a little nervous about leaving Lanell in charge of the business but Todd promised that everything would be okay. I buried my fears in the recesses of my mind. I was determined that nothing was going to ruin this trip for me. I was deliriously happy, giddy with excitement because I was almost positive that Richard was going to propose to me. The week in Ohio flew by. We built many happy memories. Then after dinner the evening before we were to leave, Richard asked for everyone's attention.

    This is it, I thought! When imagining his proposal, I had pictured us in different settings but it was always just the two of us. However, his family was very important to Richard so it didn't surprise me all that much that he would choose to pop the question in their presence.

    We were all sitting in the living room, drinking coffee. The kids were playing in a corner of the room. I was a little nervous about being the center of attention but it was a good kind of nervous. Richard began talking about our lives together, about what the kids and I meant to him. I sort of zoned out, waiting for the big moment and didn't really hear the words coming out of his mouth. Then, I realized everyone was looking at me and I wondered if I had missed his saying the words, "Shailey, will you marry me?"

    Richard continued talking and as what he was saying penetrated my brain fog, I felt a lump form in my throat. He wasn't proposing. Far from it. In fact, he was saying that he would probably never marry again and wasn't sure how much longer the kids and I would be living with him. To his credit, he did say that he loved us but he missed his privacy. He missed quiet evenings and wasn't sure he could commit to raising another family full-time.

I was stunned. Embarrassment and humiliation washed over me in waves. I wanted to run from the room but lacked the strength to raise myself from my chair. I wanted to lash out at him but the words froze in my throat. Therefore, I sat there in silence, my face red and my eyes burning with unshed tears. No one was talking now and the tension in the room was as thick as pea soup. Finally, someone suggested giving us some privacy but being alone with Richard was the last thing I wanted. I knew I would become extremely angry and I didn't want to lay into him with his family in earshot so I struggled to my feet and went to the room I shared with Salora.

I went into the bedroom to be alone and sat on the bed, mentally berating myself for once again trusting a man. How many times did I have to be made a fool of before I learned my lesson, I wondered. I didn't cry. I just busied myself with packing. At least, Richard had waited until our last night before crushing my dreams. I would have left if he had made his true feelings known earlier in the week. There was no way I would have stayed there being pitied by Richard's family.

On the flight home, I thought about what the kids and I would do. Richard and I still hadn't discussed exactly where we stood. I didn't have the money to move us to a place of our own. Every cent I had raked and scraped together for months had gone into the business. Had it been just me, I would have slept in the office but that wasn't an option.

Once the plane landed and we left the airport, I asked Richard if he could put up with us for a while longer until I could save enough to get us a place of our own. He said of course and to take all the time I needed. It was late when we got home. The light was blinking on our answering machine signaling that we had messages. I pressed the play button expecting them to be for Richard.

The majority of the messages were from the woman who was in charge of the building where I rented the office space; Holly Wilson. There was a problem and she needed to speak to me urgently. In each subsequent message, her tone became more and more agitated. The last one, she was downright rude, stating that I was in violation of the terms of our contract and that if she didn't hear from me soon she would start the eviction proceedings.

I got the kids settled in bed. I was glad it was Saturday night so I didn't have to deal with getting them to school the next morning. Even though the woman hadn't given details about what was going on, I knew that Lanell and Todd were probably behind the problems.

A quick search of some websites, confirmed my suspicions. Craigslist and other sites where ads of a sexual nature were allowed were teeming with offers of services at Blue Hands and even using the main office phone number for Cybertron. I spent the rest of the weekend trying to figure out how to put out the fires blazing the Internet and how to deal with Lanell. I didn't want to lose my business before it even had a chance to succeed.

I met with Holly Wilson, the landlord, on Monday. I promised her I would take care of everything and offered profuse apologies. She informed me that my office space would be subject to searches at anytime during the remainder of my lease. I protested but she insisted that it would be that way and if I didn't like it, the lease could be terminated early.

I fired Lanell as soon as I got to the office. I liked her but she was out of control and I knew that if I wanted to keep the business, she had to go. She had many problems, not the least being an addiction to narcotics.

I had formed relationships with some members of her family whom she had introduced me to and I explained to them that I had to let her go for her own good. Lanell needed a stable environment to conquer her addiction and as much as her working for me was causing me problems, I caused problems for her as well. The next few weeks were pure hell. Men were always stopping by. Some looking for sex and some looking for drugs. Lanell had evidently sold narcotic pills out of the office or was looking for them for herself.

These were dangerous men who carried guns and knives. One even showed up with a machete. I was terrified and had to hire a security guard to sit with me at the office for the next few weeks while the ads were removed from the web. I was furious with Todd for letting things get so out of hand. I was expecting to be busted by the police any day and was surprised but relieved that it didn't happen. This would have been the perfect time for me to kick Todd out of my life but with the uncertainty of where my relationship with Richard was going I was worried abut burning bridges, financially that is. Personally, I would have been over the moon to be rid of Todd.

Throughout the remainder of the fall, I saw clients at the office but they had to be sent to me directly by Todd. I wouldn't take any walk-ins. It was during that time that I first hired Kashawn. She had contacted me and asked if she could come to work for me and I did need some help with the office work so reluctantly, I agreed.

I had reservations about Kashawn because not only was she very young but also because she had already been in some trouble. I agreed to let her answer the phone, do filing and other things of that nature. I had decided to give her a chance and subsequently I got to meet her grandmother and parole officer.

On occasion I offered massage therapy training classes and I let Kashawn participate in the training sessions. I wanted to help her better herself so she wouldn't return to prostitution or other illegal activities. I know that sounds hypocritical but I felt I needed to protect her. At that

this whole operation was beyond scary. It was something out of a bad movie. I turned away. That anger I spoke of earlier, it had returned. This time, I went back to Alaska, emailed Todd and Greg West and told them to leave me alone. I then made arrangements for the kids and me to move out of state.

They did not take no lightly. Greg West especially. He and Todd sent me a series of emails that were very intimidating. But now I was not only pissed off I was in protecting my children mode. They were not coming near me again.

I was terrified of wondering what was next. For a long time I thought someone might show up to hurt me. I also thought that maybe I would suddenly get arrested again. I was scared that my court experiences would turn and I would end up in jail. But I was done. I don't know why I have to wait for things to get so dire before I completely walk away. However the anger and my common sense and my devotion to my faith kept me rooted and strong. I was going to change and change my life.

As of today, my children and I are doing okay. We hope to one day be able to return to Alaska as we have so many good memories as a family there. There are still the financial struggles, medical issues, and family tensions but we are together as a family which is the most important thing. Richard and I remain friends. He is close to Salora and Brice and visits us often.

Back in Alaska, the craziness still continues. The Palins' lawyers had the Anchorage Police Department issue a false press release, the police destroyed some of my property. The police claimed there was nothing they took from me that tied Todd Palin's name to mine in anyway, then later stated they never even looked through the things they took. I am still fighting with the APD. The Palins' clear misuse of their power and influence on the police and entities such as the media still continues in my life today.

The media, will not let me tell my side of the story or even comment on something they wrote in which they mention my name or refer to me. This is how I came to write this book. The following chapters hopefully allow you insight as to who I am, how exactly the Anchorage police have acted inappropriately, and how the media has played a role in my life.

Forgiveness.
When I close my eyes,
I see a candle,
fire burning inside.
Time slowly turns the years,
day by day,
a drop of rain.
The eyes of wisdom are true,
we are forgiven.
The fire washed away,
into the past.
Water, drop by drop,
dims the fire
to start again.
I close my eyes and once again
I see a flame!

© Shailey Lawes

Chapter Eight

Shailey

    A healthy, tiny little girl weighing barely five pounds was born on November 6, 1974 to Anuradha and Larry Lawes. They named this precious baby Shailey Michelle. A Hindu name mixed with a French name; a perfect merger of her parents' worlds and heritages. This baby was treasured and loved.

    Sometimes the Lawes family's home life was difficult and terrifying and sometimes it was pure joy. In her early years Shailey's family moved often. A few months after her sixth birthday a baby brother was born into their household. When Shailey was eleven, the family moved into a small town in Louisiana named Terrytown, where they settled in.

    By this time, Shailey had worked hard to develop herself academically, physically, and creatively. An avid athlete and high achiever in school, Shailey also had a deep passion for Russian ballet and had studied under world renowned leading authority Peggy Willis. Shailey was also a student of martial arts. Master Lee of Korean Tai Kwon Do in Lubbock, Texas ran an extremely traditional school. He was very strict and demanding. It was very rare a girl got accepted, but Mr. Lee not only allowed Miss Lawes into his school, he also took a personal interest in Shailey's training.

    The move to the greater New Orleans area was culturally shocking and emotionally devastating for Shailey. At that time the area did not offer the level of ballet nor martial arts training that she needed to advance in these disciplines. School was rough for her, too. She had to learn about the dark side of society-things such as racial tensions, prejudices, the violence of gangs. Once it was known that she had martial arts training, her life became a living hell. Many times she was tied up and beaten with rocks and sticks. Her grades began to slip and she became shy and reclusive.

Thinking it was the best thing for her, her father gave her permission to fight back. That changed everything; she was invited to join a gang. Saying "no thank you" was not a real option. Since no one could fight her and win, they threatened to hurt her family if she didn't cooperate. She became a member of a gang and the protector of her family.

Eventually Shailey got to study martial arts under Master Art Monroe whom at the time was world ranking 5th degree black belt in Taekwondo. She was one of his prized students. Later Shailey studied Martial arts under the guidance of the Littlejohn family and went to the Junior Olympics under their tutelage and guidance. At least this made life bearable.

Eventually her family moved into a nicer neighborhood and she was able to put some distance between herself and the gang. Reminders would appear from time to time of her obligations to the gang - tires would get slashed or someone would drop over to her new house unannounced. The only real way to escape would have been to move.

Shailey took control of the things she could control; in whatever she did, she worked very hard. Continuing to develop her skills in the martial arts, she also found time to be in the Civil Air Patrol, got good grades in school, took challenging classes for gifted students, and became a Girl Scout. She was the youngest person to have ever joined the Westbank (community) Art Guild and by the time she graduated high school she was a published poet and painter. Simply put, Shailey Michelle Lawes was an over achiever.

Her peers made fun of her accomplishments, tormenting and taunting her because she excelled. So, she went to great lengths to minimize the appearance of having developed skills and having used her talents. She denied herself any pleasure of pride, and did everything she could to appear to be in the middle range of normal. Even so, Shailey had a drive and a passion that was unmatched, and was very focused. When she could trust an adult, she shared her dreams. She was going to be an astronaut! Her doctor even wrote it down in her medical charts.

Finally, the college years arrived. At the University of Alabama in Hunstville, Miss Lawes was mentored for a short time by a famous rocket scientist (and they still correspond today). It was while attending UAH she got a rude awakening - mathematics was her enemy! She was ashamed after taking and failing the same course five times. Like many young people on their own for the first time, she needed guidance to deal with the pressure of disappointment, failure, and disillusionment. But instead of getting help, she began to isolate herself which led her into a spiral of self destruction. Shailey indulged in the college's partying life and grades slipped.

The story gets no prettier. She struggled for eight painful years. On a final exam in history, Shailey cheated, and then felt so guilty, she confessed. After that, another professor decided to carefully check the citations in one of her papers. It was not documented correctly-which the college considered a form of plagiarism. Due to the self admitted cheating and the new plagiarism charge, she was expelled from school for one year. By the time she was eligible to return to complete her studies, she was already married and living in Atlanta.

In Georgia, Shailey was busy and happy programming computers and doing some animation. Once again, she was making a name for herself for excelling in what she did, this time as a programmer and visual artist. When she and her husband bought a house in Roswell, GA, it seemed so right. She was living next to a world famous artist who became not only her neighbor and one of her dearest friends, but also became a spiritual guide. This woman, Donna Pinter, told Shailey that she must be meant for a special destiny and that she must train mentally to handle it. Shailey believed Donna had a spiritual gift of knowledge, and she looked forward to discovering what special things she would do with her own life.

Then, Shailey lost her job. Shortly thereafter, she got ill. After three months of hospitalization, she had major surgery. Her husband was not taking care of the bills while Shailey was sick. He misspent their money, and the electricity was turned off. That was the situation when she came home from the hospital. It quickly got worse; they were evicted. One year later, Shailey ended her marriage. She didn't set herself free; she went directly into another relationship. An *abusive relationship*. Her second husband became the father of her children and the tormentor of her mind. Someone she fled from, someone she repeatedly returned to. Adulthood and motherhood were confusing and heart wrenching. What had happened to the promise and potential of little Shailey Lawes?

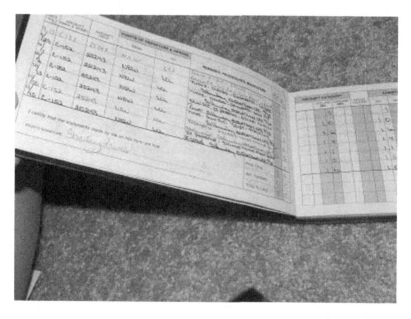

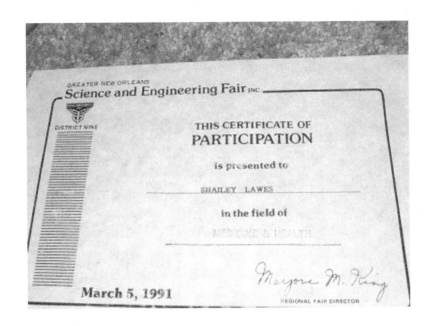

GREATER NEW ORLEANS
Science and Engineering Fair INC.

DISTRICT NINE

THIS CERTIFICATE OF
PARTICIPATION

is presented to

SHAILEY LAWES

in the field of

MEDICINE & HEALTH

March 5, 1991

Marjorie M. King

REGIONAL FAIR DIRECTOR

Desire

Hot a-flame
came thunder and
splatters of rain
cold crisp night
chills the soul
shivering under the moon
asunder
The ghost of his image
Haunts thy mind
Craving the flesh
haze
wondering when
he'll come and
take me away - - - - - - -

© Shailey Lawes

Chapter Nine

The Media & National Enquirer

By the fall of 2010 my life was returning to something resembling normal. We had left Alaska and relocated to a warmer climate, closer to friends and family that I had not seen in years. My kids were in school, happily making new friends. And then my life was turned upside down all over again. For a week straight I was suddenly bombarded with calls from reporters from major media, including the Chicago Tribune, the Star Magazine, the National Enquirer, and the New York Daily News, as well as the Anchorage Press and Anchorage Daily News in Alaska. They all wanted to know what I could tell them about my relationship with Todd Palin; things like, was it just an affair or was I his favorite prostitute. And some of them, at least, claimed to know a lot about Todd Palin; specific things like prostitution, drug use, gambling habits, and so forth. They also seemed to know a lot about me. I got the impression they were going to do a story on me whether I liked it or not.

I was scared. How did they get my name and phone number? Feeling overwhelmed, I turned to a law student friend for advice. He suggested I hire a lawyer to represent me and recommended the Foster Law Group. I spoke with Mr. Foster, who made a good first impression. I really wanted him to represent me, but he ended up referring me to his wife and partner, Kristen Foster.

I told Kristen the whole story of my encounters with Todd. I stressed to her that my primary goal was my safety and that of my children, but I also let her know that I wanted to stay out of both the press and the courts. She told me the story was most likely going to come out no matter what I chose to do, so I might as well try to get some money for my family. That way, at least something good would come out of it. As for the courts, she told me that by going public and talking to a major media outlet I would be much less likely to ever be called as a witness. That suited me just fine.

As for talking to major media, Kristen encouraged me to work with the National Enquirer, as they had a reputation for paying well. I had been contacted by someone at the Enquirer named Alan Butterfield, so apprehensively I placed a return call to Alan. From the very beginning I had the feeling something was a little 'off' about Alan Butterfield. This feeling only strengthened over time. First off, he was a big time namedropper, as if he thought that would impress me. Two names he mentioned constantly were Angelina Jolie and Sandra Bullock. I wasn't that impressed. But the namedropping wasn't the only thing that bothered me about Alan. I knew deep down he wasn't as nice as he appeared to be. Later events would confirm my intuition.

I went ahead anyway. Alan flew down to Louisiana to meet with Kristen and me, taking us to dinner at a fancy 'dress up' restaurant that Alan said was close to Sandra Bullock's house. Big whoop. We laid out my story and the evidence we had to back it up. We haggled a lot over what my story was worth and in the end I signed a contract with the National Enquirer, on September 20th, that paid me some money up front, a six figure sum once my 'exclusive' was published; and a percentage on any 'residuals' that might result from the story. It all sounded pretty good to me. I really thought that soon I would at last have a little financial security for my children and me. How wrong I was.

Once Alan left he gave me the impression he was spending a great deal of time traveling and interviewing people and verifying things. He located and interviewed three people who all independently verified my story and passed polygraph tests. Each one of these witnesses

127

eventually called to tell me what an awful experience they had with Alan Butterfield and how awful he was to them. They in turn did not want anything to do with me, nor did they even want to have to go through something like this again.

As far as his research went, Alan talked a good game. He told Kristen he had found several witnesses and also had 'anonymous' sources. I had my doubts. I gave him a long list of people to contact to verify various parts of my story, but as far as I could tell he never contacted anyone on my list.

Alan asked for various records, some to establish my personal bona fides and some to verify my relationship with Todd. I dug them out as best I could and turned them over to Alan. Richard found some of it digging through my things that were in storage at my parents' home and then met up with Alan at the Mail Boxes Etc. in Wasilla so he could copy them there. Later, when I had a chance to examine these records for myself I was astonished at what Alan had chosen not to examine or copy. For instance, there was a calendar that had notations such as "Todd" with a phone number and star next to it. There was valuable information in those records that could have also been used to corroborate my story but were not. My confidence in Alan and the ability of the Enquirer to get my story out was beginning to wane.

One point of contention became my phone records. I had several different phone numbers and knew that if those phone records were obtained they would show many calls to and from Todd Palin. From the beginning Alan was determined to get those records. I thought it would be a simple matter for me to contact the phone company and request them, but that was not the case. When I contacted the various phone companies involved, I was shocked to learn that in each instance the account information was there but the actual call information was missing.

As everyone who has ever owned a telephone knows, the phone companies keep a record of each and every incoming and outgoing call, the duration of the call, etc. A subscriber can request a copy of their call history, and law enforcement often requests this information in their investigations. But in my case, these records were simply gone—they didn't exist. Company personnel acknowledged that the records should have been there but were not, and they were just as baffled as me. Or so they said.

Alan immediately became suspicious, accusing me of lying to him and even of making up the whole thing. He berated me for it and threatened to kill the whole deal. More and more I was seeing Alan's explosive temper at work. I told him he was welcome to ask for the records himself if he didn't believe me and I happily gave him consent for that purpose. When his inquiries came up with the same result he begrudgingly admitted what I had already told him. The records had simply vanished. It was a disquieting moment. Who has the power to make phone records disappear?

Alan's investigation continued. I was given three separate polygraph tests, all done the same day in a hotel near the airport where I lived. They had a polygraph operator flown in from New York who, I was told, was a former interrogator for the FBI. He must have been good at what he did because he made me cry. Worse still, Alan shot video footage both before and after the testing, and of me hooked up to the machine with the actual interrogator present. And when it was all over the operator/interrogator told me I had passed each test beyond a shadow of a doubt. He admitted to me he had come in thinking I had lied about the whole thing, but was now convinced I was telling the truth.

Though it had been a humiliating experience, having Kristen there was a great comfort. She made notes, acting as my witness as to what the Enquirer asked me and how I had been treated. She was even allowed in the room during the actual test, on the condition she remain quiet and out of sight.

Alan let me know that he was pleased with the outcome of my polygraph testing. I think he probably had harbored some doubts about my veracity but my test results seemed to dispel his remaining doubts. But I soon learned it didn't take much to piss him off all over again. In early December, while interviewing people to verify my story, Alan spoke to a former nurse who had assisted the owner of the spa where I had massaged Todd and Sarah Palin.

I had purposely not told him about massaging Sarah out of respect for her privacy and, besides, I did not feel it had anything to do with my association with Todd. So when Alan learned this information he called me, hoping to 'set a trap.' He asked me repeatedly if there was anything I was holding back. He told me I ruined my credibility and the interview the Enquirer had done with me earlier. When they had asked me if I knew Sarah Palin, I had answered no. Was I lying to him?

I insisted that I didn't know Sarah. I felt I had to honor my client's confidence. When he finally realized I was not going to admit knowing her, he revealed what Heather Tipikin had told him about my having massaged Sarah. He then lashed into me, telling me that just proved how dishonest I was. I was devastated once again. Ironically I'd tried to protect Sarah Palin's privacy and maintain some semblance of integrity and the result ended up as I now was regarded as a liar and not credible.

When he had calmed down somewhat, Alan requested details of the Sarah Palin massage:

From: Butterfield, Alan
<AButt(redacted).com>
Subject: sarah palin massage
To: "alaskapctechy@yahoo.com"

<alaskapctechy@yahoo.com>
Cc: "kristen@(redacted).com"
<kristen@(redacted).com>, "Levine,
Barry"blevine@(redacted).com>
Date: Saturday, December 4, 2010, 9:47 AM

Shailey
Please outline the circumstances and give a
narrative surrounding you giving sarah palin a
massage at 'all about you.'
thanks
Alan

 I responded as best I could.

From: Shailey Tripp
<alaskapctechy@yahoo.com>
To: AButterfield@(redacted).com; alan b
<abenq@(redacted).com>;
kristen@(redacted).com
<kristen@(redacted).com>
Sent: Mon, Dec 6, 2010 2:16 pm
Subject: Narrative of Massage given to Sarah
Palin

I barley remember giving Sarah Palin a massage.
It happened on a day I went to work at All About
You to collect a paycheck from the chiropractor
I worked for. The person suppose to do the
massage didn't show. I was asked to fill in. The
pay for that massage came from All About you
not the chiropractor. I didn't even know who the
client was going to be literally until I walked in the
room to introduce myself. The massage was

uneventful as far as I can remember. I have not spoken to Sarah Palin before that massage or anytime after that massage. I can't even place the exact time frame of when the massage happened other than once she had a baby everyone in the All About You clinic was really shocked as no one knew she was pregnant.

Shailey

As the year's end approached I was getting more and more nervous about the story's publication. Why hadn't the Enquirer printed anything yet? Kristen and I both asked when the story was going to appear. What was taking so long? Alan finally told me the Enquirer was concerned about legal liability, but that made no sense to me. Alan Butterfield had been working on the story for several months, interviewing witnesses, and gathering records. I had been vetted from here to Sunday. I had passed their polygraph tests with flying colors. Why didn't they publish my story?

Because it had something of a history of getting stories wrong, the Enquirer had good reason to be reluctant about running my story. Joe Coscarelli, who writes a blog for the Village Voice, summed it up pretty well:

The only cred the *Enquirer* has, especially when it comes to political affairs, is left over from the John Edwards and Rielle Hunter nonsense, which to be fair, they owned months before any legitimate media outlet. But by now, with countless miscues in between, that should be wearing thin, especially considering it's the same publication that pushed a Barack Obama affair only to retract the report right away. How long can we really hold out hope that nailing Edwards

132

was a savvy act of journalism that could be repeated and not a broken clock being right?[1]

Todd and Sarah Palin were major public figures. I guess they were at a point where they couldn't afford to screw up this time. Anyway, Alan kept putting us off.

Meanwhile, in about December 2010 or January 2011, as I waited for word on the Enquirer story, a trusted media contact put me in touch with a man named Geoffrey Dunn. Dunn told me that at an appropriate time he wanted to interview me and perhaps help me write a book. I had no idea who Dunn was then, but he was a respectful, kindly man. He seemed legit.[2] Dunn somehow knew I was under contract with the Enquirer. As we spoke I learned that not only did he know Alan Butterfield, he liked and respected Alan as well. "Alan and I are very good friends," Dunn told me.

We ended the conversation on a cordial note, agreeing to pursue this further once the Enquirer story came out. Dunn insisted that I let Butterfield know he had contacted me in order to reassure Alan that he was not out to steal the story.

Less than twenty four hours later I got a call from my media contact who was highly upset with me for upsetting Dunn. My contact told me Dunn was devastated and that it was the first time he had heard a grown man cry. Of course I pressed for details. I was told Dunn had apparently been chewed out by Alan and had even been physically threatened. I immediately called Dunn up to offer my personal apology. Right away I heard the strain and hurt in his voice.

"I have never been threatened and talked to the way Alan Butterfield talked to me," Dunn told me. "Don't ever contact me again. There is something about you that is very dangerous and I don't want you anywhere near me."

I apologized and promised I would never contact him again. We ended the conversation in what I felt was a respectful way, but when I hung up the phone I began to cry. I felt so sorry for this kindly old man. I felt like I was the one who had hurt Dunn even though Alan had done that. That is when it hit home to me how underhanded and mean Butterfield really was. Whatever he said to Dunn, it had really upset him. Kristen later told me I should never have apologized, but I'm glad I did. He seemed like a really nice man who had children to care for. My heart went out to him.

I found out later through my media contact that my apology had meant a lot to Dunn, which was gratifying. And as I watched events unfold that fall and winter I became more and more disillusioned with media in and how it operated. I was beginning to see how freely people were manipulated, facts twisted, and lives altered, not for the sake of the truth but for quick profit. Frankly, I had never seen so much childish behavior in grown adults.

We continued to push Alan for word on the story. Finally he told us that they were set to publish but before they could go forward they had to tell the Palin lawyers what they had. I didn't understand that at all but deferred to the 'legal' people about that stuff. So we sat back and waited some more.

From: kristen@(redacted).com
[kristen@(redacted).com]
Sent: Monday, December 27, 2010 4:47 PM
To: Butterfield, Alan
Subject: Any progress on the Palin story?

Hi Alan:
I hope you had a wonderful Christmas and that you have something good planned for Friday night. Shailey is feeling pretty anxious about the status of her story. Any news from Palin's camp?

Have you contacted him about the story? Is there anything else that you need from Shailey? Thanks.
Take care,
Kristen

-------- Original Message --------
Subject: RE: Any progress on the Palin story?
From: "Butterfield, Alan"
<AButterfield@(redacted).com>
Date: Mon, December 27, 2010 3:20 pm
To: "kristen@(redacted).com"
<kristen@(redacted).com>

So far nothing. Palin's camp has denied the story and have challenged us to provide them with documents.
Shailey's phone records she claimed to have had would have been useful.
Hopefully I'll have more of an update later this week.
Alan

It came as a surprise to no one, least of all me, that they denied the story. It irritated me that Alan brought up the phone records, since he himself knew they had disappeared. But that was Alan.

Alan had been telling me that one way the story could come out with the concern about legal liability from the Palins was if a third party source revealed the affair. Then, bam! Almost miraculously, as if Alan's big Christmas wish had come true, on January 4th an anonymous email was sent from thepalinmorals@hotmail.com to various media outlets, including the Enquirer. This anonymous informant wrote:

"My sources reveal that a massage therapist and computer technologist, SHAILEY TRIPP, had an affair with Todd Palin that lead (sic) to her arrest March of 2010. According to the tenants in the building of her offices, they saw Todd come and go often and heard noises that sounded like someone was having sex. It was the same tenants who called the police on her."

Alan Butterfield was ecstatic about this "coincidental" turn of event. The Enquirer could now publish a story about me and attribute it to an anonymous source and therefore relieve themselves of the threat of a lawsuit by the Palins.

From the outset I was suspicious about this mysterious "source." After Alan had expressed so much concern about running my story, about lawsuits, and all the rest of it, the sudden appearance of this "anonymous source" seemed way to convenient. I wanted more than anything to know the real identity of the person or persons behind the cryptic email. I was never to have that opportunity, for while numerous national media printed the contents of this "anonymous source," I was never able to get my hands on a forwarded copy of the email itself, from which I might have been able to track its origin.

For his part Alan tried hard to get me to say I thought the author was Kashawn or Amber or someone else I knew. But I couldn't do that. At any rate, Alan said they were now ready to publish something and it would be soon. I was now more apprehensive than ever, even as I was relieved that my story would finally see the light of day. On January 7th Kristen sent Alan what was essentially an ultimatum.

From: kristen@(redacted).com
<kristen@(redacted).com>

Subject: publication
To: "Alan Butterfield"
<AButterfield@(redacted).com>
Cc: "Shailey Tripp"
<alaskapctechy@yahoo.com>
Date: Friday, January 7, 2011, 9:51 AM

Alan:

Shailey has been informed by friends and family that there are a number of journalists and others trying to find her. In addition, she has learned that there are a lot of rumors about her on the internet that simply are not true. She is getting nervous that her side of the story is not coming out, and we need confirmation from you that the Enquirer is going to print the story within the next two weeks. If the Enquirer can't give us this confirmation within 24 hours, then Shailey will explore other avenues for making sure that her side of the story is told. The Enquirer has had this information for over three months, and at this point, it seems as though the Enquirer has no intention of publishing the story. Shailey can't continue to put her life on hold. She remains hopeful that the Enquirer will publish but is getting more doubtful by the hour. Shailey wants this to work with you, but she doesn't want to miss her opportunity to be heard. Thanks.

Kristen

Then on January 19th I was startled to learn that the Enquirer was trying to alter our deal, as seen in this email exchange between Kristen and Barry Levine, executive editor of the National Enquirer:

From: Levine, Barry
Sent: Wednesday, January 19, 2011 3:27 PM
To: 'kristen@(redacted).com'
Subject: Second new separate deal with Shailey Tripp

Kristen:
I thought the story in the new issue "Sarah Palin's husband caught up in sex scandal!" looks very good on the cover, which is circulating now in NY and LA. A small tease will be put up on our website in the morning.

We are very happy with the separate deal, and would like your approval on a second one for this coming week as Alan has discussed with you. This would pay Shailey $2,500 (two thousand five hundred), per same CMO arrangement in order to keep story hot on our cover for a second straight week. The new story would include some new arranged photos with Shailey and also detail from a quoted source that Sarah Palin once came face to face with Shailey when Shailey gave her a massage. The story would say that the massage took place at the same location where Todd had received a sexual massage from Shailey only weeks before.

This story, like the one in this week's issue, is separate from our agreement signed Sept. 20, 2010. Of course, I hope these stories build interest leading to us publishing the big one!

Best regards,
Barry Levine
-------- Original Message --------

Subject: FW: Second new separate deal with Shailey Tripp

From: "Levine, Barry" <blevine@(redacted).com>

Date: Wed, January 19, 2011 3:27 pm

To: "'kristen@(redacted).com'" <kristen@(redacted).com>

Cc: "Butterfield, Alan" <AButterfield@(redacted).com>

Kristen—In addition to the $2,500 for the new story as proposed below, we will also pay Shailey $1,000 (one thousand dollars) for allow Alan Butterfield to shoot new photos of her in Louisiana. It's extremely important that we're all on the same page with this and you agree to this asap so we can move quickly as we're on deadline for our next issue – and it's in all our best interests to keep the heat on this story!

Please approve asap.

BL

. . . .

From: kristen@(redacted).com <kristen@(redacted).com>

Subject: RE: FW: Second new separate deal with Shailey Tripp

To: "Levine,Barry" <blevine@(redacted).com>

Cc: "Butterfield,Alan" <AButterfield@(redacted).com>

Date: Wednesday, January 19, 2011, 2:21 PM

Barry - Shailey was hesitant to agree to this second separate deal because she has several concerns. Ultimately, however, I believe that we have the same goal - publication of the exclusive with Shailey, and I expressed to Shailey that these separate teaser articles are being pursued and published in a good faith effort to build interest in the story and to shake the tree up in the hopes that additional people or documents are revealed that provide further verfication of the exclusive. Given what Shailey went through with Todd, it is easy to see why Shailey is worried about being used. Nonetheless, based on my conversations with you and Alan, I feel comfortable assuring Shailey that you are acting in good faith and that your ultimate goal is the same as her ultimate goal - both parties want to see the exclusive published and the original contract fulfilled. Therefore, Shailey is in agreement with the second separate deal as set forth below. We hope that this will lead to the publication of the exclusive with Shailey in the near future. Thank you for your hard work on this.

Take care,
Kristen

Needless to say, I didn't like the way the contract discussion was going but I still had faith in the way Kristen was representing me. Anyway, on January 21st the *Enquirer* story finally hit the newsstand, and they did it in their usual fashion, with a two-page spread under the banner headline, TODD PALIN SEX SCANDAL!

No subtlety there. The gist of the story was that Todd Palin had cheated on Sarah with a female massage therapist who was "busted for prostitution" and named me as that person. According to the story, an anonymous e-mail tipper suggested that this affair is what led to my arrest in March 2010. *The Enquirer* claimed to have "uncovered" official documents that I was arrested for maintaining a house of prostitution and that the cops had confiscated evidence that could tie Todd to the alleged extramarital affair.

This was apparently what they call a 'teaser' story in the tabloid business. When I saw it I had many mixed feelings. I felt relief that my story was finally out, even though it really wasn't. I felt that even though the whole story—the story I wanted told—had not yet been published, this was a start. Surely now, I thought, the mainstream media will jump on the story and get to the truth on their own. How so very naïve I was.

Alan tried to allay my concerns, insisting that his follow-up story would feature more details. He got me excited by telling me that he wanted to send a photographer to do a photo shoot for the follow-up story. When he flew down, though, he was by himself. After recording another interview, he dropped me off to get made up and then took me shopping for the shoot. He wanted me to pick a name brand store like Macy's but that would have meant a long drive and there was no way I could travel that far and be home in time for my kids, so we went to JC Penny's instead. It was a nightmare. He was so rude and awful to the sales clerk that I was embarrassed to be with him. It bothered me so much that I went back the next day and apologized to her. Alan had treated her like he expected her to wait on us hand and foot, to an extent that was horrifying. She appreciated my apology.

Alan shot some photos at the store and other ones outside. He took them in a way that made them appear candid, as if I were under surveillance, but of course they were totally staged. And although they had pictures of me that I thought made me look terrific, they seemed to select photos that were the least flattering.

Further confirmation of Alan Butterfield's creepiness came not long afterward. Despite his promise to my attorney and me that he would not contact my 'ex' or his family because it might endanger my kids and me, he did it anyway. I have since heard from many of them and they all let me know Alan was the one who had contacted them. What a guy.

The day before the follow-up story was scheduled to run I got another shock when the Enquirer posted the following at its online site:

LATEST UPDATE: 9:15 PM EST 1/25/11
The Anchorage Police Department have issued the following press release:

Shailey Tripp Investigation APD #10-1823

The Anchorage Police Department investigation and arrest of Shailey Tripp has recently been mischaracterized in internet blogs and in a National Enquirer article. Several errors regarding the investigation and arrest were reported in the Enquirer article (printed and internet versions):

*None of the physical evidence examined by police showed any connection to Wasilla resident Todd Palin and his name did not appear in any of the records seized by APD.

*The investigation of the prostitution operation was initiated by Anchorage Police Department's Vice Unit responding to internet advertisements, not through information developed from any tips or other persons.

*No Rolodex was seized and taken into evidence.

*The National Enquirer has not contacted Anchorage Police Department Public Affairs Unit to fact check its story so their reported "call to Anchorage Police Department" could not have been returned.

*"Bloggers" have had no access to the evidence seized so their linking of evidence in

police custody to any other person is incorrect.[3]

My head started spinning. This so-called "press release" was riddled with inaccuracies, and the Anchorage cops had sent it directly to the *National Enquirer*. What the hell was going on?

Things began to happen fast after that. The following day, before the Enquirer piece hit the streets, the New York Daily News[4] published the following story on its online site:

Todd Palin, husband of Sarah Palin, is not involved in a prostitution ring with Shailey Tripp: cops

BY ALIYAH SHAHID
DAILY NEWS STAFF WRITER
Wednesday, January 26, 2011
Looks like the First Dude is off the hook.

The Anchorage Police Department blasted the National Enquirer's recent report that Todd Palin is embroiled in a sex scandal involving an extramarital affair with a massage therapist who belonged to a prostitution ring.

"It was just guilt by innuendo, nothing else," Lt. Dave Parker told the Daily News on Wednesday. "There's not one scintilla of evidence that Todd Palin had anything to do with this."

The Enquirer claimed 36-year-old Shailey Tripp was arrested for maintaining a house of prostitution in March and that cops had confiscated physical evidence that could tie ex-Gov. Sarah Palin's husband to the alleged affair.[5]

It was almost too weird to be real. The "First Dude" was "off the hook" based on the say-so of one cop? Not only had the Anchorage Police Department issued a press release whose intent appeared to be to discredit me, someone with the APD was actually commenting to the media in a partisan way. Lt. Parker's "guilt by innuendo" comment certainly seemed, to put it mildly, subjective. Further down in the story there was yet another juicy quote from Parker. Shahid wrote: "In explaining the bombshell allegations, Parker said some in Anchorage were just 'rabidly anti-Palin,' adding 'they will do anything to destroy the platform Sarah Palin is standing on.'

For all intents and purposes the APD had entered the political realm to kill the story—my story.

While still trying to process that information, I hurried down to Wal-Mart to pick up a copy of the new Enquirer piece. The headline blared out:

TODD'S ACCUSER SAYS SHE MET SARAH FACE TO FACE

Oddly, the tabloid had made my routine massage of Sarah Palin, which Alan had grilled me about a month before, the focus of their story. There was a nice, big paparazzi style photo of me talking with a cup of coffee in my hand. Otherwise, the story was a rehash of the prior story.

Sarah Palin reacted quickly. That same day–January 26–she appeared on the Bob and Mark Morning Show in Anchorage and used the APD press release, as well as Parker's comments to the New York Daily News to refute the story in the media, as reported the following day by ABC News.

Sarah Palin Defends Husband: Prostitution Ring Accusations Were "Big Lie"

ABC News' John Berman reports:

For the first time, Sarah Palin weighed-in on the report from the National Enquirer linking her husband Todd to prostitutes in Alaska.

Appearing on the "The Bob and Mark Morning Show," a radio call-in show in Alaska, the former Governor said, "What hurts are the lies that come from Alaskans."

She noted that the Anchorage Police Department (APD)

144

denied the Enquirer story. " Look at this recent BS about Todd supposedly being all caught up in a prostitution ring in Anchorage. And then APD had to come out and say bull, there's no evidence."

Indeed Lt. Dave Parker of the APD told the New York Daily News "It was just guilt by innuendo, nothing else...There's not one scintilla of evidence that Todd Palin had anything to do with this."[6]

What was particularly striking was the way Parker's press release and separate comments to the press dovetailed so nicely with Palin's own response. But I hadn't seen anything yet. Soon after the second story appeared my lawyer, Kristen Foster, dropped the bombshell that the Enquirer wanted to rewrite my contract! The Enquirer's contention that our contract was not binding until they had published an "exclusive" about me, and because the two stories they had published so far were based on other sources, the contract had not yet kicked in. It suddenly explained, at least in part, why the Enquirer had been so careful to not to use their extensive interviews with me, replying instead on the 'anonymous source' email, my arrest, and my seized property being held at the APD.

The Enquirer's offer to "renegotiate" my contract by giving me a few thousand dollars instead of the original six figures was met with appropriate derision by Kristen, as can be seen in this exchange with Barry Levine:

From: Kristen Foster <KFoster@(redacted).com>
   Subject: Palin
   To: "blevine@(redacted).com"
<blevine@(redacted).com>
   Cc: "alaskapctechy@yahoo.com"
<alaskapctechy@yahoo.com>
   Date: Wednesday, January 26, 2011, 2:26 PM
   Barry:

Shailey is absolutely not willing to take less than the $120,000 from the original contract. Based on the story that went out today that uses quotes from Shailey but attributes the quotes to a "pal," Shailey is entitled to the full amount due under the original contract.

Shailey feels that the Enquirer has used her and treated her poorly. She is irate. Her family has been put through a great deal emotionally as a result of this story and the information that the Enquirer has disclosed about her. This story is worth far more than $120,000. Shailey will not accept less. Because of the unprofessional behavior of the Enquirer, Shailey wants to be paid in full within the next five days or she will initiate a lawsuit in Florida for breach of contract.

Kristen D. Foster

From: Kristen Foster <KFoster@(redacted).com>

Subject: Palin

To: "blevine@(redacted).com" <blevine@(redacted).com>

Cc: "Shailey Tripp" <alaskapctechy@yahoo.com>

Date: Thursday, January 27, 2011, 7:03 AM

Barry:

I got your message from last night, and I appreciate that you don't want to send emails back and forth. Unfortunately, your offer yesterday was so insulting that it is important for Shailey to be involved directly with any further communication, and there really is no need for back and forth emails. We simply need to know if the Enquirer intends to fulfill its obligations under

the original contract and will guarantee payment in full to Shailey within two weeks from the publication of yesterday's article.
    Kristen D. Foster
    From: Kristen Foster
<KFoster@(redacted).com>
    Subject: Palin
    To: "Levine, Barry" <blevine@(redacted).com>
    Cc: "Shailey Tripp"
<alaskapctechy@yahoo.com>
    Date: Friday, January 28, 2011, 10:57 AM
    Barry:
I have spoken with Shailey, and she told me that Alan had called her. Our position has not changed. The publication of the article on Wednesday that directly quotes Shailey and attributes those quotes to a non-existent "pal" constitutes publication of the exclusive under the original contract. There is no basis for the article other than the interview with Shailey for the exclusive, and the Enquirer is obligated by the contract to pay Shailey in full on or before February 9, 2011.
    Thanks,
    Kristen

Once I was sure the Enquirer had breached our contract I began giving interviews to bloggers that I felt had some credibility. After the fiasco with the National Enquirer I was desperate to tell my story in my own way. If the national media would not touch my story, perhaps a blog would. I knew that some of the more popular bloggers had many thousands of followers. I felt it was worth a try.

    This will already be old news to anyone familiar with

the blogosphere, but blogs about Sarah Palin are quite
numerous and there is a crystal clear dividing line between
those that are pro and the anti-Palin, with the pro-Palin
forces being for the most part rabidly conservative and the
anti-Palin people predominantly liberal. There was
obviously no way a pro-Palin blogger was going to go near
me, so I turned to blogs that I felt would be interested but
that would also deal with my story in a fair manner.
The first interview I did was with Jessie Griffin who runs a
political blog called The Immoral Minority. After some
initial email exchanges I became satisfied that Jessie would
be fair. We did a telephone interview that I thought went
quite well. Jessie posted the audio online and the vast
majority of commenters felt I sounded credible. That came
as a big relief. I finally felt vindicated. At last the public
was hearing the real story. The interview was soon posted
to YouTube and had over 10,000 hits.

My next interview was with Malia Litman, who
publishes a well-respected blog by the same name. Besides
writing insightful political commentary, Malia also
happened to be an attorney. I liked that. Malia interviewed
me on February 10th and posted a summary on her blog the
next day. She summarized our contacts this way:

Having communicated on the phone with
Shailey for an hour, and having exchanged e-
mails, it is my personal opinion that Shailey is an
honest, hard working, and a dedicated mother.
As a single parent she is committed to revealing
the truth about the Palins. It is her hope that one
day her children will know that in spite of less
than ideal circumstances, pressure, and the
potential financial gain of "selling" her story, she
volunteered the story to those who she trusted to
report the truth.[7]

Not only did Malia interview me, she went the extra

148

mile to investigate what no one else in the media was willing to look at or even talk about: Lt. Dave Parker's notorious press release. With a lawyer's determination she began calling the Anchorage Police, Municipal Prosecutor, and anyone else who might listen. Her hard work paid off. Malia interviewed Lt. Parker, getting him to admit that he was "the person responsible for the Press Release issued to the National Enquirer."[8]

The Municipality of Anchorage maintains a website that is used by its various departments, including the police department. One of the things the APD does is post press releases to its website. Malia proceeded to set up Parker as well as any seasoned attorney could. Under her skillful questioning Parker said, "issuing press releases is part of his job as the "Public Information Officer" and explained that the police department has a "Web Master" who determines the content of the web site. Parker then admitted he never sent the National Enquirer Press Release to the Web Master for her consideration to include in the public web site.

The question of course is why did Parker not want this press release made public even though he had sent it to the National Enquirer? But the best was yet to come. Parker then told Malia that after the National Enquirer story about me was published; Sarah Palin's attorney – whom Parker believed was Thomas Van Flein – contacted the APD and asked them to review their records, and if there was not a mention of Todd Palin's name, to then issue a press release to that effect. Dave Parker, being the Public Information Officer at APD, was given this task.

Parker told Malia that before issuing the press release he reviewed the records pertaining to my arrest that were "readily available to him" on his computer. He spoke to Sergeant Cathy Lacy and the Vice Squad. He also reviewed some seized paperwork including "loose leaf" notebooks that contained client names and numbers, and although he thought that computers and cell phones were seized, he made no attempt to review any information on any of them. Thus if Todd Palin's name or phone number appeared on these computers or the cell phones, he would not have known. In other words, Parker confirmed to Malia that he did not have all the information when he prepared the press release for the National Enquirer. Parker also admitted to Malia that no one with the APD had checked my computer or cell phone records, or those of Kashawn Thomas, reminding me how my own phone records had mysteriously disappeared. He did say that "Rabid" anti-Palin people might try to "conjure" something up. He did confirm that the cell phones and computer would be returned when both cases are closed, and that there would be no reason for any phone numbers or names to have been deleted.[9]

Lt. Parker later called Litman to clarify that he had not spoken to Thomas Van Flein, but rather John Tiemessen, Sarah Palin's attorney of record in Alaska. Malia posted that Parker, who reads her blog, had not disclaimed or repudiated any of the statements attributed to him, either in phone calls or emails.

To me, Lt. Parker's pro-Palin bias flowed from every line in his press release, his interview with Malia Litman, and his comments to the press. Following the APD press release, the New York Daily News, and ABC stories, other media quickly followed, reporting that the story about myself and Todd Palin, and my reputation, had been discredited. Media representatives that had wanted a comment or story from me following the initial *National Enquirer* story suddenly would no longer talk to me. A planned follow-up story by the *Enquirer* was cancelled, I believe as a direct result of the false APD press release.

The list of television and internet personalities and entities that contacted me eagerly wanting a story, only to pull back almost immediately, reads like a 'Who's Who' of entertainment media: AshleyMadison.com, Laura Novak, Radar Online, Star Magazine, a writer with the AP Wire, and, yes, even the New York Times. I know for a fact that at least some of these sources dropped any consideration of telling my story because of what they were told about me by Alan Butterfield. Actually, the media I had contact with seemed to fall into two camps: Those that said I had a 'credibility problem,' i.e. Alan Butterfield told them I had a credibility problem, and those generally more mainstream media who really wanted to run my story but who said that bosses wouldn't let them. In other words, "We're afraid to run the story because the Palin's might sue us." What does that say about the state of media and the free press?

The experience left me jaded about the role and functioning of our media today. I could see now that taking my story to the National Enquirer had been a monumental mistake. Perhaps I even should have expected it. But what can you say about the media out there? How is it possible that one media source will take the word of another without first doing their own due diligence? Once the Enquirer refused to honor my contract, all the media who were initially interested in my story but who later dropped the idea because of what they 'heard' about me, not one was willing to hear what I had to say for themselves, examine the documentation I had, independently question witnesses, or polygraph me. To put it bluntly, the National Enquirer blacklisted me.

But I have even more distaste for the so-call legitimate media like the New York Times. These folks know what I had and that it was valid information. There were investigations being done of the high level prostitution going on in Alaska. It was known that these activities potentially implicated some very powerful people. And yet, to date, not one media outlet has had the guts to tell this story. Not one. When our media—or perhaps it would be more accurate to say those corporations who own our

151

media—are afraid to tell the American people, I fear that our democracy is in a lot of trouble.

They say spring is a time of hope and renewal, but by the spring of 2011 I felt defeated. My hope of getting my story told while providing for my family was quickly fading. To add insult to injury, around this time I began receiving an increasing number of anonymous emails like this one:

Hi!

I just wanted to say that I applaud you for your bravery. However, I must say that if you continue, you will destroy at least one innocent life. I know you've seen your share of tragedy. But please reconsider future action. Do you really want to cause someone as more (sic) or more pain than you've ever felt in your entire life?

Ask yourself, is it worth it?

Warm regards

Not only did the media not want to tell my story, no one else wanted me to tell my story either. I asked myself, could things get any worse?

I was about to find out.

[1] http://blogs.villagevoice.com/runninscared/2011/01/todd_palin_had.php

[2] I learned soon after that Dunn was an award-winning writer and filmmaker. In May 2011 he released *The Lies of Sarah Palin*, published by St. Martin's Press.

[3] http://www.nationalenquirer.com/celebrity/todd-palin-sex-scandal-alaska-cops-issue-statement

[4] According to Wikipedia, the New York Daily News is the fourth most widely circulated daily newspaper in the United States (see:

http://en.wikipedia.org/wiki/Daily_News_(New_York))

[5] http://articles.nydailynews.com/2011-01-26/gossip/27737965_1_todd-palin-prostitution-ring-sarah-palin

[6] http://abcnews.go.com/blogs/politics/2011/01/sarah-palin-defends-husband-prostitution-ring-accusations-were-big-lie/

[7] http://malialitman.wordpress.com/2011/02/11/exclusive-interview-with-shailey-tripp/

[8] http://malialitman.wordpress.com/2011/02/22/the-anchorage-police-admit-misstatements/

[9] http://malialitman.wordpress.com/2011/02/22/the-anchorage-police-admit-misstatements/

153

Remember

I open my eyes,
gaze into the hazy sky
The sun a-flare
as I smile and inhale the sweet air.
I am filled with love, warmth, and glee
a sense of wholeness within me....

© Shailey Lawes

Chapter Ten

The Anchorage Police

Kashawn Thomas and I were arrested March 4, 2010 at my place of business, Cybertron & Blue Hands. I employed Kashawn as an independent contractor. This was a large raid with fourteen or fifteen officers participating. There were two men wearing jackets with FBI patches. I believe there were also representatives from Homeland security present. I was told it was some kind of joint task force. Before they arrested me, an APD officer interrogated me. I believe this was Detective McKinnon. The officer claimed that the police had my office under video surveillance for the past two months.

During this interrogation, I was asked if any "big name" politicians had come to my office. He mentioned by name Ted Stevens, the Murkowski's, Sarah Palin, and Todd Palin. The questions began to focus on drugs and under age sex trafficking. Did I know anything about public figures engaging in these forms of illegal activity?

I confirmed that Palin came to my office. I was not asked any more questions about Todd Palin at that point; they moved on to asking about other politicians and businessmen. They named names. When I did not respond, he turned off the recorder and asked Kashawn Thomas if I was keeping her hostage as a sex slave or forcing her to do things she did not want to do. Where was that coming from? Thank God Kashawn didn't make things up to please them, she said no.

When they took me into custody, a number of items of my property were seized by the APD. A list of these items is included in the Appendices section of this book; as are other documents I will mention in this chapter.

I pleaded no contest on June 13, 2010 and a hearing date was set for June 15, 2011. At the hearing, after it was shown that I complied with all the terms of my probation, my case was dismissed by Judge Pamela Washington. The return of my property was then discussed at some length. The judge ordered all of my property returned with the full consent of Municipal Prosecutor David Wallace. The sole exception was cash - two hundred six dollars.

Given the judge's order, and the prosecutor having given his consent, I anticipated a swift return of my property. Matt from the municipal prosecutor's office assured me that the return of my property would be expedited and told me to expect my property back within seven to ten business days. Maybe that would have been true in someone else's case, but it was not how it worked out for me.

There ensued a frustrating two-month period of phone calls while I attempted to obtain the return of my property. During this time individuals at the APD stalled by claiming that they were waiting for the paperwork or authorization from the municipal prosecutor's office. I believed it for a while, but subsequently learned this was not the case.

Matt at the prosecutor's office assured me that they already sent to APD all of the necessary paperwork and authorization they needed to release my property. I was both angered and disappointed to learn that the APD was not honest with me and they were not forthright in dealing with my property.

As part of my efforts to obtain the return of my property I contacted Judge Washington's clerk for assistance. Through a series of phone calls I learned that Judge Washington's clerk had contacted both the municipal prosecutor's office and the APD and had told both to comply with the judge's order. The APD ignored her.

At length I was contacted regarding the return of property. After repeated attempts to reach him by phone, I received a phone call in the middle of the night from Detective McKinnon. He told me I would be getting all of my property back. He said he had been alerted about four months prior that my property contained "controversial information" and needed to be handled with special care. He wanted to assure me that none of the electronic information had been looked through and that he did not look through my cell phones, credit card machine, or computers. Also at this time he confirmed I would get everything back on the property and seizure list except for any money and possibly not the condoms.

Three weeks later I arranged for my mother to pick up my things after preparing a power of attorney for her. When my mother and a witness, Jesse Griffin, showed up at APD to pick up my property an APD employee, I believe her name is Cara, would not release everything to them. When Cara was informed about my conversation with Detective McKinnon (in which he assured me all my things would be returned), she told my mother that is not what her paperwork indicated. Pressed further, Cara said the fault was with the municipal prosecutor.

My mother relayed this information to me, I called the prosecutor and as before, I was assured that I was to get all of my property returned except for the money. When this information was repeated once more, to Cara, she changed her story and stated it was the judge's fault. I then called the judge's clerk and was assured that the judge had not modified the order in any way. When Cara was asked yet again, to release my property, she became agitated and said that it would have to be taken up with Detective Parker.

Cara and I had spoken prior to this. Her response in the past was that it was the Judge and the City Prosecutor's order to not let me have the other items. She insisted that I get a specific court order by the judge to let me have that stuff. Cara was nice and polite and repeatedly told me she can't wait for all my things to be picked up and that the APD was probably more anxious to get rid of it than I was eager to get it.

Blogger/lawyer Malia Litman reported that in the early morning hours of October 31, 2011 she received a call from Detective McKinnon who told her that after her previous call to him (some months prior) he personally went to the Evidence Department of the APD and advised them to be "extra careful" about not losing the evidence because there might be a lot of controversy regarding this evidence. McKinnon also told Litman that he had issued the paperwork necessary to allow the release of all the "evidence seized" in the Shailey Tripp matter.[1]

Was there a disconnect at APD with regard to the disposition of my property? Detective McKinnon, who worked my case, stated clearly that ALL of my property except for the cash would be returned, while on the other hand Lt. Parker and Cara (acting on instructions from Lt. Parker) insisted that not all of my property could be returned. I believe someone at APD provided Cara with incorrect information about the disposition of my property; specifically with regard to what Judge Washington and the municipality had clearly stated and documented with regard to my property. I believe this person was Lt. Parker.

It is now February, 2012 and the APD is continuing to withhold personal property of mine in defiance of Judge Washington's order and my constitutional rights. The APD was aware of the judge's order and of the municipal prosecutor's concurrence in its return. And most significant, the case officer, Detective McKinnon, told me that all my property was to be returned. As far as I can tell only Lt. Parker insists that APD cannot return it all. I have yet to be given any valid reason or excuse as to why.

Based on my conversations and contacts with the various players involved, I believe that Lt. Parker and possibly other persons within APD have an agenda separate and apart from their duty as officers which causes them to be protective of one or more persons whose names they believe are contained in the property being withheld. The further proof of this is the bizarre issuance of a press release by the APD in January, 2011.

On January 21, 2011 the supermarket tabloid *National Enquirer* reported that Todd Palin cheated on Sarah with a female massage therapist who was "busted for prostitution." According to the story, an anonymous e-mail tipper suggested that this affair is what led to my arrest in March 2010. *The Enquirer* claimed having "uncovered" official documents that I was arrested for maintaining a house of prostitution and that the cops had confiscated evidence that could tie Todd to the alleged extramarital affair.

The Palin story supposedly originated after several media outlets received an anonymous e-mail from thepalinmorals@hotmail.com claiming that I had an affair with Todd. The source of this email has never been identified.

Four days later, and one day before the *Enquirer* was scheduled to run a follow-up story, the tabloid posted the following at its online site:

LATEST UPDATE: 9:15 PM EST 1/25/11

The Anchorage Police Department have issued the following press release:

Shailey Tripp Investigation APD #10-1823

The Anchorage Police Department investigation and arrest of Shailey Tripp has recently been mischaracterized in internet blogs and in a National Enquirer article. Several errors regarding the investigation and arrest were reported in the Enquirer article (printed and internet versions):

*None of the physical evidence examined by police showed any connection to Wasilla resident Todd Palin and his name did not appear in any of the records seized by APD.

*The investigation of the prostitution operation was initiated by Anchorage Police Department's Vice Unit responding to internet advertisements, not through information developed from any tips or other persons.

*No Rolodex was seized and taken into evidence.

*The National Enquirer has not contacted Anchorage Police Department Public Affairs Unit to fact check its story so their reported "call to Anchorage Police Department" could not have been returned.

*"Bloggers" have had no access to the evidence seized so their linking of evidence in police custody to any other person is incorrect. [2]

As will be seen, most if not all of the information contained in this "press release" was either inaccurate or misleading. And, significantly, it was not posted on the APD public affairs web page in the customary manner as other APD press releases.

The release was sent to the *National Enquirer*, which published it, as noted above. The following day, January 26, the New York Daily News[3] published the following story on its online site:

Todd Palin, husband of Sarah Palin, is not involved in a prostitution ring with Shailey Tripp: cops
BY ALIYAH SHAHID
DAILY NEWS STAFF WRITER
Wednesday, January 26, 2011

Looks like the First Dude is off the hook.

The Anchorage Police Department blasted the National Enquirer's recent report that Todd Palin is embroiled in a sex scandal involving an extramarital affair with a massage therapist who belonged to a prostitution ring.

"It was just guilt by innuendo, nothing else," Lt. Dave Parker told the Daily News on Wednesday. "There's not one scintilla of evidence that Todd Palin had anything to do with this."

The Enquirer claimed 36-year-old Shailey Tripp was arrested for maintaining a house of prostitution in March and that cops had confiscated physical evidence that could tie ex-Gov. Sarah Palin's husband to the alleged affair.[4]

The same day – January 26 – Sarah Palin used Lt. Parker's press release and his comments to the New York Daily News to refute the story in the media, as reported the following day by ABC News.

Sarah Palin Defends Husband: Prostitution Ring Accusations Were "Big Lie"

ABC News' John Berman reports:

For the first time, Sarah Palin weighed-in on the report from the National Enquirer linking her husband Todd to prostitutes in Alaska.

Appearing on the "The Bob and Mark Morning Show," a radio call-in show in Alaska, the former Governor said, "What hurts are the lies that come from Alaskans."

She noted that the Anchorage Police Department (APD) denied the Enquirer story. " Look at this recent BS about Todd supposedly being all caught up in a prostitution ring in Anchorage. And then APD had to come out and say bull, there's no evidence."

Indeed Lt. Dave Parker of the APD told the New York Daily News "It was just guilt by innuendo, nothing else…There's not one scintilla of evidence that Todd Palin had anything to do with this."[5]

It is clear from the above that Lt. Parker deliberately interjected himself into a national story with the objective of defending Todd Palin and destroying my credibility in the media. This is exactly the result that was achieved.

In an attempt to sort this out, blogger/attorney Malia Litman obtained an interview with Lt. Parker and on February 22, 2011 posted on her website the contents of conversation she had with Lt. Parker.[6] According to Litman, Officer Parker confirmed that he is the person responsible for the Press Release issued to the National Enquirer. He explained that issuing press releases is part of his job as the "Public Information Officer." He explained that the police department has a "Web Master" who determines the content of the web site. Mr. Parker never sent the National Enquirer Press Release to the Web Master for her consideration to include in the public web site.

Officer Parker indicated that after the National Enquirer story involving Todd Palin and Shailey Tripp was published, the Anchorage Police Department was contacted by the attorney for Sarah Palin who he believes was Thomas Van Flein. The attorney asked them to review their records, and if there was not a mention of Todd Palin's name, to then issue a press release accordingly. This task was given to Dave Parker as the Public Information Officer.

Before issuing the press release Dave Parker reviewed the records regarding the arrest that were readily available to him on his computer. He spoke to Sergeant Cathy Lacy, and the Vice Squad. He also reviewed the paperwork that he perceived was the paperwork seized. He was not aware of, and did not review, "office calendars" but he did review "loose leaf" notebooks that contained client names and numbers. He thought that computers and cell phones were seized, but made no attempt to review any information on any of them. Thus if Todd Palin's name or phone number appeared on the computer or the cell phones, he would not know. He didn't mention any photography in the information reviewed. Of course if pages had been removed from the "loose leaf" notebooks, he would have no way of knowing about that.

Subsequently I phoned Lt. Parker and he indicated there seemed to be some confusion about the case number on the computer he was using, and indicated he would need to do further checking and would call me back. He did call back and confirmed that there is a police number and a

163

court case number.

Officer Parker confirmed that Officer Billiet was the officer who had spoken with William Fortier when the initial call was made regarding possible prostitution activities. Dave Parker did not know about Officer Billiet's involvement or his tip from William Fortier. Thus Dave Parker confirmed that he did not have all the information when he prepared the press release for the National Enquirer. Officer Parker confirmed that no attempt was made by him, and to his knowledge, by anyone with the Anchorage Police Department, to check the computer records or cell phone records of either Kashawn Thomas or Shailey Tripp. Thus he confirmed that the names of many people could be on the computer or cell phones seized, but he would not know about that. Thus if Todd Palin's name appeared on the cell phone or lap top of Shailey Tripp, Officer Parker was not in a position to confirm or deny that. He did say that "Rabid" anti-Palin people might try to "conjure" something up. He did confirm that the cell phones and computer would be returned when both cases are closed, and that there would be no reason for any phone numbers or names to have been deleted.[7]

Lt. Parker later called Litman to clarify that he had not spoken to Thomas Van Flein, but rather John Tiemessen, Sarah Palin's attorney of record in Alaska. Lt. Parker, who according to Litman reads her blog, has not disclaimed or repudiated any of the statements attributed to him by Litman, either in phone calls or emails to her or to me.

I also draw your attention to the fact that Lt. Parker's pro-Palin bias is readily apparent, not only in his interview with Malia Litman but also in his utterances to the press. Following the APD press release, and the New York Daily News and ABC stories, other media quickly followed, reporting that the story about myself and Todd Palin, and my reputation, had been discredited. Media representatives that had wanted a comment or story from me following the initial *National Enquirer* story suddenly would no longer talk to me. A planned follow-up story by the *Enquirer* was cancelled, I believe as a direct result of the false APD press release.

The above shows that Lt. Parker, using the color of his authority as the APD press officer, "cooked up" a press release that he knew or should have known to be inaccurate, at the request of Sarah Palin's attorney, to create the false impression that the department had cleared Todd Palin of wrongdoing on and, perhaps more importantly, "kill" a story that Parker and Palin's lawyer calculated could be damaging to the Palin's. In so doing, Lt. Parker damaged my credibility.

Based on the above, I conclude that Lt. David Parker, acting at the specific direction of Sarah Palin's attorney, John Tiemessen, knowingly issued a false and misleading press release for the purpose of aiding Sarah Palin politically, and Todd Palin personally, and that in doing so he violated the ethical standards of a police officer and brought discredit to the Anchorage Police Department. I also believe that Lt. Parker has conspired to withhold personal property seized from me, in direct contravention of APD policy and Judge Washington's order, out of belief that he is aiding Sarah Palin politically and Todd Palin personally. For these reasons I believe he is unfit to wear the uniform of an APD officer. It is also possible, although I have no direct proof, that others at the APD may have aided Lt. Parker in the above effort.

I have also reported the above information to the Internal Affairs Division of the Anchorage Police Department. I have not received a response from them except to say that they have opened an investigation, only to refuse to investigate only a few weeks later. In my letter to APD Internal Affairs I stated that I was seeking the following:

165

- The return of ALL my property as ordered by Judge Washington
- A full investigation of the circumstances of my property being withheld and appropriate punishment of any person at APD who acted improperly or illegally with regard to my property
- A full investigation of the APD press release that was issued about me, to include the full circumstances of its issuance, determination of whether it was politically motivated, and appropriate punishment of any person at APD who acted improperly or illegally with regard to this press release
- An official and public retraction of the press release to correct/repudiate the falsehoods contained therein, and
- A letter of apology to me for the stress and humiliation that has resulted

Frankly, I am not expecting a fair and impartial investigation by the APD.

Lastly, I sent Judge Washington updates and have filed several motions in November and December 2011. The latest information I have is that the APD reported to the Alaska Court System that my remaining property was destroyed on September 14, 2011. Is that true or is it another lie? I have no way of knowing. I am waiting to see what the court will decide to do about these actions by the APD in direct defiance of a court order.

In addition I was further notified by Ryan from APD Internal Affairs that there were no grounds for an investigation. Ryan "knows Parker personally" and says Parker is just "a good ole' guy" and "he didn't mean any harm" and that Parker "can be very literal" and "we can't hold that against him." Ryan concluded that the APD stands firmly behind Parker and his actions. When I asked about the inappropriate email Parker sent to me, Ryan's response was well you are a prostitute and you were charged with running a house of prostitution. When I informed him that all my charges were dropped and that I felt demoralized by Parker's letter he assured me Parker meant nothing by it and again reminded me that I did admit I was a prostitute. I could see this conversation was non productive so I ended the conversation. Ryan is suppose to get back with me to let me know if the APD will grant me the same treatment as the Palins and will let me submit my own press release for Parker to publish. That was December, 2011; I am still awaiting an answer.

[1] http://malialitman.wordpress.com/2011/10/31/the-missing-evidence-seized-in-the-matter-of-shailey-tripp/
[2] http://www.nationalenquirer.com/celebrity/todd-palin-sex-scandal-alaska-cops-issue-statement
[3] According to Wikipedia, the New York Daily News is the fourth most widely circulated daily newspaper in the United States (see: http://en.wikipedia.org/wiki/Daily_News_(New_York))
[4] http://articles.nydailynews.com/2011-01-26/gossip/27737965_1_todd-palin-prostitution-ring-sarah-palin
[5] http://abcnews.go.com/blogs/politics/2011/01/sarah-palin-defends-husband-prostitution-ring-accusations-were-big-lie/
[6] http://malialitman.wordpress.com/2011/02/22/the-anchorage-police-admit-misstatements/
[7] http://malialitman.wordpress.com/2011/02/22/the-anchorage-police-admit-misstatements/

My Myth

I am the courage, the leader, the warrior
I am the decision maker, the caretaker
Strong in mind - body - soul
Stronger than I know
She will come to touch me
as I am to prepare
Destined to journey far into the darkness
beware of fear and jealousy for they will
stalk you
but share your burden with sweet
husband (family)
For in the soul, so delicate, fraile
Your child self sits...waiting for your
protection
as the world waits too...
For I am young and have started a
journey
and the legacy awaits
as I wait to learn
Myself through guidance and help
If I seek the way
It will come!

©Shailey Lawes

Chapter Eleven

Witnesses

Along the road of these crazy and intense experiences in my life there have been many people who have witnessed some of these events. Most people will not step forward. They have their reasons - job safety, personal safety, and avoiding being ostracized in their hometowns and communities. However a few people did try to step forward for me and their courage and unselfishness is worthy of mention.

First there was Heather Tipikin, a work friend and associate. We are casual acquaintances and when we worked together we got along well. Ours is not a deep and binding friendship but we are friendly. Heather is a person of integrity and was raising her younger sister on her own. Heather worked at the All About You Spa, and her exact title is unknown to me but I believe she was a medical assistant, CMA (Certified Medical Assistant). Whatever her credentials, she was the owner's right hand.

The Enquirer found Heather Tipikin and interviewed her. It went beyond an interview. They interrogated her and humiliated her and gave her harsh treatment as if she was some lowly liar with an agenda.

Heather did not deserve that kind of treatment. She had no connection to my business dealings with Todd Palin, but she did know I had given Sarah Palin a massage and knew that I had given Todd Palin a massage at the spa where we both worked. Heather Tipikin was polygraphed by the National Enquirer and found to be credible. She further validated that no one in the office knew Mrs. Palin was pregnant. It was not a personal attack on Sarah Palin. None of us wanted anything about Sarah Palin to come out in the media. Heather, like myself, is not a doctor, and we at the time had no idea the significance of what we were saying. She and I were told over and over again to just tell the truth. I think Heather might have thought, as I did, that Sarah Palin was indeed pregnant and never thought to challenge the fact that maybe she wasn't. It is only now after everything that I have been through that I, myself, understand the significance of Heather and me both stating that we did not know Sarah Palin was pregnant when she visited the spa.

Another person to note is Enri S., a personal promoter in Anchorage. We became acquainted through another mutual friend. Enri and I became casual friends and kept up with one another's lives but we did not hang out daily or talk that often. Enri knew I was a prostitute. He also knew I was smart and he encouraged me to continue my work toward my undergraduate degree. The shady part of my life was not a secret from those close to me - that is the point I am trying to make.

One day Enri came out to my office to visit and possibly go to lunch. It just happened to be a day and time that Todd Palin was waiting for me and Enri recognized easily the Governor's husband, the "First Dude." When my story broke he decided to tell the Enquirer what he had witnessed. The Enquirer interviewed him relentlessly and polygraphed him. As far as I know he passed the polygraph just fine.

Kashawn Thomas also verified parts of my story. She told the Enquirer that she knew Todd Palin and I had sex, admitting that one time she even listened to us have sex in the office. She also confirmed that he would only see and speak to me and once waited hours for me.

Three other important sources are the people who phoned in the prostitution complaint to the Anchorage police, ultimately leading to my arrest - Lauri Jorgenson, William Fortier, and Rachel Broady. In their statements, they told officers they had seen Todd Palin coming in and out of the building many times and heard loud and inappropriate noises when he was in the office that sounded to them like sex. They thought he was seeing me for sex. They also said they'd found used condoms in the dumpster behind the building.

Finally, there is Amber C. This woman is also from a mixed family background similar to myself and was a martial artist when she was younger. Amber had achieved a lot in her life but nevertheless was homeless and trying to hold multiple jobs in an attempt to change her situation. Obviously, we had a lot in common. Amber worked for me for many months and became a close and trusted friend. She also had seen me with Todd Palin many times. Amber did nothing to hide her dislike of Todd from me. She knew Todd and I had sex and did not approve of it at all. She felt certain he would hurt me one day. Many times she told me to get him out of my life because he would lead me to getting arrested. I am no longer in touch with her as we parted ways cordially after my arrest in March of 2010.

Based on the interest of the various members of law enforcement asking me about Todd Palin before my arrest, Todd's own behavior brought attention from the police. Exactly what they heard from others beyond these witnesses I've named, I cannot say. What I do know, is that the people I've named told different media outlets their stories and what they witnessed. As far as I know their credibility was never in question. What was in question was whether or not they would be slapped with a lawsuit by the Palins. It boggles my mind that when many people are willing to step forward and tell the truth, that the truth can still be buried or bent or distorted. None of the people above have any reason to lie for me nor have I encouraged them to do so. But they did see many other people lie about me. They saw how I was mistreated by the police, and how the Palins have used their influence to bury the story. I like to think their motivation to state what really happened was to set the record straight.

I hope that after reading this book many others will come forward. There are others who have known Todd in the way I once knew Todd. I've met a few of them. I met them through Todd, himself - women and men in the same position that I was in when he brought us together. If any of them read this, I hope they, too, will gain the courage to come forward or at least start making more positive changes. Everyone should be able to live without fear, but until they get out of the prostitution business, they will be shackled by it. My advice to all of them is to move away, get counseling, and accept help to change your life. It is not easy. You will need an incredible support system, but if you look for it, you can find it.

I just want to say to all of you who did come forward and stood by my side, thank you. The cost to you was huge and I know that. Thank you for doing the right thing.

Wondering

Going through the sands of time
Living everyday with joy
Listening to heaven's chime
Perfect harmony persists -
Balance and divine tranquility is
the sorrow's end
Perfection and abstract views
from the eyes
Contend dew drops falling

one
by
one

drip

drop

The new times begun.

©Shailey Lawes

Chapter Twelve

Interviews with Shailey Tripp

Sometimes when we read a story we get caught up in characters and plots but miss some of the foundation. When writing this book we decided to include an interview section. An interview asks direct questions and can be a great way to obtain information. In the past when I granted an interview I was restricted somewhat by what I could say due to my open court case. Now I have more freedom to answer questions more openly and honestly and that is in part of how this book came to be. Therefore in this section three interviews have been included for your review. The first interview presented here was with Jesse Griffin. This interview took place after my deal with the National Enquirer fell apart. The next interview I placed here was with a blogger identified as Blade from Shesnohockeymom blog spot. Lastly, there is a brand new interview with me and the co author of this book, Vickie Bottoms. I have done a total of five interviews thus far. Four of those can be found on the internet on the Immoral Minority blog, Malia Litman blog, shesnohockeymom blog, and Chris world blogspot.

Transcript of Interview with Shailey Tripp
Originally published on Immoral Minority Blog – Feb 11, 2011
(http://theimmoralminority.blogspot.com/2011/02/here-is-transcript-of-my-interview-with.html)

JG: Hi Shailey, how you doing?
Shailey: Hi, good.

176

JG: And for uh, for um, for this interview could you go ahead and state your full name for me?

Shailey: Yes. It's Shailey Tripp.

JG: OK, thank you very much and, and by the way thank you very much for your time.

We really appreciate that you're taking the time to answer some questions for me.

According to the National Enquirer you had a relationship with Todd Palin. Is this an accurate statement?

Shailey: Yes, that is correct.

JG: Mm, hmm. And was this relationship sexual in nature?

Shailey: Um, yes it was.

JG: And about how long did this last?

Shailey: It started probably in early 2007 until um, about the end, December of 2009.

JG: OK, and during that time, during that time or after that time even did you ever have a chance to meet Sarah Palin, the governor?

Shailey: I did. Um, I had formerly met her at a place that I had worked at.

JG: Uh huh. And can you describe how that encounter took place?

Shailey: Um one, one day when I went to that particular work to pick up a paycheck, um, the massage therapist that would have worked that day didn't show up and basically they just asked if I wanted to make some extra money that day and if I would have time to give a massage. And I said yes and um, I had, had no clue who it was or anything like that until I had walked into the room and that's, that's how I met Sarah Palin. I had gave her a massage once, just one time.

JG: Now this place is the All About You Spa and uh I went there to see what the, what

the criteria were and there were some health screening paperwork they had available
there for their clients. Do you know whether or not Sarah Palin had to fill out the same
kind of paperwork?

Shailey: Yes, she definitely would have had to fill out that same paperwork.

JG: So all the questions on there she would have had to filled out including when was her last period, whether or not she was pregnant, whether she was receiving any kind of
medications and, and so on and forth. Correct?

Shailey: That is correct.

JG: Mmm hmm..

Shailey: And the same things to get a massage...so she would have had to have that
paperwork filled out prior to getting a massage.

JG: So you would have seen that paperwork before you gave the massage.

Shailey: Yes. During what I typically...what I typically do is just go in meet the person
before I do anything to that person, ask them a few questions, go out of the room. If I
think they had medical things I needed to look over or if the doctor would had flagged the chart I would have taken a few minutes to wash my hands, read the chart and then go back in the room.

JG: OK, did you as her any questions before you began the massage?

Shailey: Um, I did. I always ask every patient, especially a female patient three questions
before I begin the massage. Her heart wasn't flagged, so I didn't really look over the
notes in detail for what was going on with her but I did ask her if she was pregnant, I
asked her if she was on any blood thinners, I asked her if

178

she thought there was anything
I should know about her health before I began the massage.
JG: When you asked if she was pregnant, what was her response?
Shailey: She said, "No."
JG: She said no. And, um..I'm sorry, I don't think I asked you this question. When did
this, um, massage take place?
Shailey: Um, I want to say that it happened in the end of February, early March of 2008
but it definitely happened between January and the beginning of March of 2008.
JG: So some time in that, that time period. OK.
Shailey: Yeah.
JG: OK, so…So you asked that question and she said, "No."
Shailey: That's right. Yeah.
JG: OK. Now, during the massage, what was the state of her, of her, of her.. (laugh) I
mean, how much was she wearing during the massage, I should say?
Shailey: Um, well, usually, most women keep their underwear on and cover up with a
blanket. In this case she would have covered up with, uh, she was covered up with a sheet
and like a thicker blanket. Um, the way I remember it was that she just had her underwear
on and I know that because when I came back into the room to give her the massage she
was lying facedown, which means your head is in a face cradle looking down and, you
know, you're laying on your stomach and, um, I began the massage on her neck and
upper back. Um, and I remember that because I remember that being a complaint of hers
was that her neck was really hurting.

179

JG: Her neck was really hurting… Now was she laying, um facedown on the, on the
table?

Shailey: Correct, yeah.

JG: She was. OK. Now you know, if you gave a massage in either January or February,
she would have been about, from what we understand, five to six months pregnant?
Maybe seven months pregnant? Did she appear to be pregnant…

Shailey: …(inaudible)

JG: …to you when you looked at her?

Shailey: No, she didn't appear to be pregnant and I had no reason to think that she was
pregnant.

JG: No reason whatsoever?

Shailey: No, not at all.

JG: Have you ever, or had you at that time ever given a massage to women who were
pregnant?

Shailey: Yeah, several.

JG: Several. And is there a different procedure you go through? A different approach
that happens when a woman's pregnant?

Shailey: Yeah, it's really, really different. Um…Where you touch them, how you touch
them, um, even the way they lie down. They would never lay on their back, I mean, on
their stomach or straight on their back. You would, you would have special pillows. You
would use a special massage table or you would prop them up a special way on their
side…In some women's cases they have to sit in a chair and receive a chair massage. It
just depends on the woman and their pregnancy. But you wouldn't lay them typically in a

laid out position on their backs or on their stomachs.

JG: (inaudible) Um, when you massaged her, did you have, um did you give her a

massage anywhere around her abdomen area?

Shailey: I did. Uh, that was another complaint. She just said that, um, her stomach was

really sore and um, I didn't do a firm massage and I wouldn't have had the sheet or the

blanket all the way off her chest where I could see her naked, but I would have pulled the

paper blanket down and left the sheet kept on around her and then um, with light pressure

rubbed her stomach.

JG: But you would have felt her entire stomach, abdomen area. Is that correct?

Shailey: That is correct.

JG: OK, I'm going to ask you to kind of make a judgment call here. While you were

massaging her abdomen, was there anything about that that indicated to you that she

might have a child, or have a fetus inside of her?

Shailey: No, nothing at all. I was just concerned because of how tender she was and I

remember just letting the um, the nurse know after that I thought maybe she might have a

urinary tract infection and had I let her know that too..

JG: Oh, really?

Shailey: Yeah, because she was, she was really tender. But her stomach wasn't rounded

or firm and there was no movement in her stomach at all to indicate that there was a baby

in there. And I really…I was really, really shocked when she announced that she had had

a baby a few months later.

JG: OK, a few months later, OK. Um, and was..were you the only one shocked in the office or was everyone pretty shocked?

Shailey: No (scoffs) the whole entire office was shocked and talked about it for a number
of days and there were a lot of hurt feelings in the office and people were just really
upset.

JG: Why were they upset?

Shailey: Um, I can't speak for them but I just think they just felt a sense of betrayal by a
patient and just shocked because no - nobody knew that they - that she - was pregnant
and I think she just would have been treated in a very very different way, especially like,
I'm the one that gave her a massage that time and um, I know she'd been seen for a few
other procedures in the office and I just think everybody was concerned and, um...

JG: Were some of those procedures...

Shailey: I think more...

JG: I'm sorry. Go ahead.

Shailey: I just think more than anything people, people were just really, really shocked
because they had no clue that she was pregnant.

JG: Now were there some procedures that took place, that took place in that spa that
would not have been given to a woman who was pregnant?

Shailey: Yeah, there's several, several things in the spa that would not have been done to
somebody who was pregnant, or if they would have been done they would have been
modified.

JG: Do you have, do you know for a fact if she that she might have had some of those
treatments?

Shailey: I know for a fact she did but I can't say what they were.

182

JG: Oh, I…yeah…

Shailey: I can just state that I gave her a massage because I'm the one that gave her the
massage.

JG: I understand that. I understand that. Did she continue to to, um, to come there to that
spa after ah, your massage? I mean, did she come for other procedures afterwards? Did
she come for other massages afterwards?

Shailey: I believe she had another checkup…

JG: Uh, huh…

Shailey: …um, shortly after that, about two weeks after that. And then I don't think she
had come back to my knowledge I don't think she had come back to the spa.

JG: OK, so around March or so…and she definitely - and she definitely did not come
back again after she announced her pregnancy, is that correct?

Shailey: That's correct.

JG: So her next visit would have been before she announced that she was pregnant.

Shailey: Right…

JG: And yet still, when she made the announcement, nobody in your office or nobody in
that area, in that spa, had any idea that she was, uh, with child.

Shailey: No, nobody. Um, In fact, two people cried. They were that upset that they cried.
They were really upset.

JG: Out of a feeling of betrayal or for fear that they might have done something to harm
the fetus?

Shailey: Probably both. Probably more a feeling of a state of shock but also afraid that
they could have hurt her or the baby.

183

JG: OK, that is very interesting information by the way. Um, let me ask you a question
going back to the Todd Palin, uh, part of this. Um, how, how often would you say you
and Todd got together for sex, altogether?

Shailey: Um, it's hard to put a number on it. It's not like a crazy number but um, I
probably saw him about every other month, um, over the course of almost three, a full
three years I'd say at least a minimum of twelve times.

JG: So twelve times, OK. OK, Shailey, I think that's going to pretty much do it for us.
And, and let me ask you another question…there is more information that you have at
your disposal about um, Todd Palin and your, and your relationship with him and other
things that happened is that not correct?

Shailey: That is correct, yes, and that is in a legal situation.

JG: Right. But you are hoping to get that story out.

Shailey: Yes. Definitely.

JG: Very good. OK. Well thank you very much for..oh and I'm sorry before I…and you
do have documentation to back up much of what you are saying, is that also correct?

Shailey: That is correct. Yeah.

JG: OK, well thank you very much…

Shailey: …I have lots of copies…

JG: Go ahead.

Shailey: I'm sorry. I just was saying I have lots of copies to back up what I'm saying. So
I don't retain the only copies.

JG: OK, well thank you very much for your time Shailey. I really appreciate that.

Shailey: Thank you for calling. OK. Bye-bye.

Interview conducted by online personality Blade from Sarah's Scandals
http://shesnohockeymom.blogspot.com/2011/02/interview-with-shailey-tripp.html

Blade: Hi, Shailey. I appreciate your granting me this interview. I already know a little about you from my research. Here is the background information I have for you. Is anything incorrect or would you like to add anything? You are 36 years old and originally from Louisiana. You are divorced from your second husband and raising two special needs children, a boy and a girl, on your own. You are a licensed massage therapist and also held a manicurist license. You do computer programming and enjoy writing poetry and short stories among other things.

Shailey: My Dad was military and we moved often. I consider Louisiana my home state and I did complete high school there but I was born in North Carolina.

Blade: When and why did you move to Alaska?

Shailey: I moved to Eagle River, AK in 2002 with my first husband. Later in 2002, I moved back to Huntsville, AL. I went back and forth between Alaska and Alabama until 2004. In April of 2004, I moved to Alaska as my permanent home. I still visited Alabama, trying to repair my second marriage. All contact with my second husband ended in the fall of 2005. I believe I have kept a driver's license, voting card, and my business license in Alaska from 2002 until the summer of 2010.

Blade: Did you live in Wasilla? If so, when? If not where did you live?

Shailey: I lived in Wasilla, AK from February 2005 until early September 2006. Then in November of 2006, I lived in Palmer, AK. From May of 2009 to May 2010, I lived in Anchorage, AK.

Blade: When did you first meet any member of the Palin family? Who was it and under what circumstances? How would you describe their attitude? Friendly? Uppity? Holier than thou?

Shailey: I first met a member of the Palin family in late November or early December of 2006. I met a daughter at a public school I was subbing at. I was a recess monitor and lunch monitor for 3 days.

On one of those days, this daughter was causing a problem in the lunch line. I scolded her, placed her in a time out and then made her go to the end of the lunch line. In the gym after lunch, she was a little mouthy. Very typical teenage behavior, nothing really crazy. I sent a note to her parents. The next day her father came to school and had the daughter apologize. He also offered an apology. We casually talked. He told me that his name was Todd. I told him mine was Shailey and that I worked at a nearby hair place that offered tanning, manicures, and massages. I was the massage therapist. That is how it all began. It was very casual. Nothing weird. I didn't say anything to him that I wouldn't say to any other person I was meeting for the first time. I only remember it because of the way he was dressed, his manners, and because of what the relationship became.

Blade: When and where did you first meet Todd? How long after you met Todd did your relationship become sexual? Was your relationship with Todd different than with other clients? Did he ever confide in you? What brought about the end of your relationship with him?

Shailey: That is a good question. I already answered how I met Todd and how our relationship began in the previous question. My relationship with Todd was different from other clients because we had sexual contact. That was the first time this happened to me in this context. I want to let you know right upfront that the first time I lived in Alaska, I worked in a very upscale place. The women there taught me that you could take your shirt off to give a massage and earn extra money. It was even encouraged but no one

186

wanted to "know" about it. So I was predisposed to the idea, but was very shocked when it happened. I heard rumors but didn't believe that kind of thing really happened.

After about three massages with no incidents or anything, weird things started to happen. At first it was a lot of wiggling on the table and some noises, which he hadn't done previously. He was lingering and making a point to touch my hand. In fact, I think this happened the 3rd time (the noises, lingering , and touching my hand).

Then the next time, at the end of the massage, he rolled over onto his back and asked if that was it. He then placed my hand on his penis and asked if I could help him out a little. I thought I was going to die. He immediately said nice things to me and offered an extra $50.00 to $100.00. I did what he wanted.

Then it progressed to, "Well, you did this last time. Can you take your top off this time?" Eventually, it led to sex. If that is what he wanted he provided the protection and he left with it. He always paid an extra $50.00 to $100.00 and he always took anything he used with him. Also, he really did want the massage. Weird, huh? Always. After about 6 months he started to refer what he called "business friends" to me. Sometimes he paid for them in advance, cash only, and those men would also leave $50.00 to $100.00. Sometimes he would drop the money by in an envelope. The first time he did this the girls in the shop teased me. The first time he sent someone to me, I honestly thought it was a referral to help me. A legitimate referral. When I realized the man wanted more than a massage, both he and I were stunned that the other didn't know what was going on. He was even angry.

Blade: Sometime during Sarah's gubernatorial campaign you donated some gift certificates and products that you thought were for a real estate agency. Was that the Kristan Cole agency? Were the gift certificates for massage services? How long are gift certificates for massage services valid?

Shailey: I do not remember the agency. I think it was along the lines of the owner of the shop said she was gathering donations for such and such a cause. She named what she was donating and asked could we all match her. There was a big real estate convention at the time and a real estate agent picked up the donation. I remember her saying the donated items were going in thank you gift bags. Yes, the gift certificates once used came back to me, and yes it would have names on them and dates used. No, I can not give you that information at this time.

Blade: You said you gave Sarah Palin a massage sometime between January 2008 and March 2008. Are you certain it was in that time period? Was that the first time you had ever seen her in person? If not did she appear different to you in any way?

Shailey: I am certain. I lean towards the February - March 2008 time frame. No, it wasn't the first time I had seen her in person but it was the first time I had any personal encounter with her. No, I met her while she was laying face down.

Blade: You asked Sarah if she was pregnant before starting the massage and she said no. Did she hesitate or was it an assertive no?

Shailey: She said no. Her answer didn't raise any red flags for me. I had no reason to doubt her.

Blade: You said that Sarah was laying on her stomach on the massage table. Did she seem to be in any discomfort while in that position?

Shailey: She seemed fine to me other than it seemed like it was hard for her to relax. To her credit, that is not unusual for your first massage with a person you don't know.

Blade: You stated that you massaged Sarah's abdomen so at some point she had to move from her stomach to her back or side. Which position was she in for the abdominal massage? Did she have any difficulty changing positions?

Shailey: This particular massage started facedown, which means she laid on her stomach. Then mid way I had her turn over so she was laying on her back. She seemed able to do this without assistance and made no complaints other than her stomach was sore.

Blade: Did you notice anything about Sarah during the massage that indicated she was pregnant? Was there anything about her that seemed unusual? Approximately how long did the massage last? Did Sarah make small talk with you? If so do you remember anything she said?

Shailey: Again, I had no reason at anytime to think she was pregnant. I was more worried that she was going to confront me and get me fired than I was about anything else. I did remember her shoes. The massage lasted approximately 50 minutes. She wasn't a talker other than indicating what she needed me to work on or asking me to adjust pressure. I was just happy when it was over and hoped that she got something out of it because I felt it was the worst massage of my life.

Blade: After you finished the massage, did you remain in the room while Sarah got down from the table? If yes, did she request any assistance? When you've given massages to other pregnant women do they usually ask for help getting on or off the table?

Shailey: I did not assist her getting on or off the table. I left the room after telling her to remain laying down. I washed my hands, then got water and took it to her. I advised her on a few things and left the room to give her privacy to get up and get dressed. I charted my notes and left. Usually, I stay to talk to a client after giving a massage but in this case, I left and went to the break room.

Blade: At any time did you see Sarah in a standing position while not fully clothed? If so did she appear to be carrying any extra weight in the abdominal area? Did you observe her walking? Was there anything suggestive of pregnancy

189

in her gait?

Shailey: No, I don't think I saw her in a standing position that day.

Blade: Do you know if Sarah used a gift certificate for the massage that you gave her. If so do you know if it was one of those that you donated?

Shailey: No, she did not use a gift certificate. I was paid for that massage through either the doctor or the nurse I worked for. I would have to really research that to know how I got paid for that massage. I do not know how she paid for this service.

Blade: Did you and your co-workers learn of Sarah's pregnancy prior to the birth of Trig? If so what was the general reaction? What was the reaction to her traveling from Texas back to Alaska to have the baby? Was there talk about it being a dangerous thing to do?

Shailey: One day in the break room, the radio was on. They said Gov. Palin had a baby and we were all like, "What?". Shortly after another worker came into the office talking about her having a baby and we were all just shocked. It seemed to us that she had recently been in, (meaning within the past month or 2) and none of us had a clue. We were shocked! We did pay attention to the news on this subject after that. I remember a small T.V. in the break room but it was taken out after we all misused it. I did not know about that trip until last week. I have been doing some reading up on the curiosity of her being pregnant. I had no idea that it was a big deal or that any theories on her pregnancy existed. When I was 20-something weeks pregnant and needed an angel flight they almost didn't fly me so I am unclear as to how she was able to fly on a commercial flight.

Blade: Did you ever hear rumors about Bristol being pregnant in early 2008? If so what did you hear?

Shailey: I heard rumors that summer and that fall if I remember correctly. I heard them at a beauty shop I worked at in the valley; not at any of the clinics I worked at.

Blade: Is there anything that you would like to add about your experiences with the Palins or about yourself?

Shailey: I still feel a little mystified as to why anyone would care that I gave her a massage other than because of her celebrity status. Anything that took place between me and the Palins was really a minor event in my life compared to other things that were happening to me personally. These interactions took place at a time in my life when I was in extreme hardship and was trying to rebuild my life from that hardship. Also, my kids needed a lot of medical attention and that is where my main focus was. I really do not know anyone in that family other than Todd.

That concluded the original interview but I had some follow-up questions for Shailey. Her responses to those questions are below.

Blade: The place where you first gave Todd massages, was that AAY Spa or another place? If it was a different place, did your sexual relationship with Todd begin there? Did Todd follow you when you began working at AAY and after that when you had the office in Anchorage?

Shailey: The place I first gave Todd a massage was another place. There are several of these kind of places all over the area. The name of the place I first gave Todd a massage at was xxxxx, and later, there was a massage at ooooo. However, this time was so congested and so many things were happening that I am not 100% sure if I had sex with him at xxxxx. I think I saw him there for his initial massage. Then at ooooo (the original location which later moved), I had sex with Todd for the first time. I am not sure these shop owners would want their businesses' names published but I mentioned them so you are clear. Also, ooooo and xxxxx are physically very close to one another. At some point xxxxx went out of business.

Blade: When you say that you remember Sarah's shoes,

can you explain what you mean? What was memorable about them?

Shailey: I love shoes!!! I fantasize that I, in my daily life, wear ultra high heels. The truth is I am clumsy as hell and they hurt my feet. The aunt I admire most can play basketball in her heels. Anyway, there were several times I was in Wasilla shopping for shoes and all of the women's shoes were not available because Sarah had bought them all. So naturally when she came for a massage, I admit I did check out what kind of shoes she was wearing. She had on these amazing 6 inch taupe heels. I have no idea what brand of shoes they were but I loved them and me being me, thought it was kind of funny that she wore them.

Blade: Do pregnant women usually request assistance getting on or off the table?

Shailey: Pregnant women always ask for assistance getting on and off the massage table as do geriatrics. Most importantly, if I know a woman is pregnant, I have a special stool for them to use and also a special way I like to position them. Sometimes I even offer a chair instead of a table. Additionally, I would never do certain types of massages on a pregnant woman due to blood pressure issues and possible labor.

Blade: So you weren't aware of Sarah's announcing her pregnancy the first week of March? You didn't hear any of the talk about her not looking pregnant?

Shailey: No, I was not aware of her announcing her pregnancy ever.

Until a few weeks ago when Jesse Griffin came into my life I had never heard anything about her being pregnant and certainly not "conspiracies" about her pregnancy. This is news to me and a little silly. If anything I thought she was pregnant and horribly selfish for the things she did to her body while she was pregnant. It never occurred to me that she wasn't pregnant or faked it. It still seems absurd to me because I can't relate to it at all or even understand a motive for it.

Blade: After learning that people believe Sarah faked her pregnancy in 2008, what is your personal opinion? Do you believe Trig is her and Todd's son?

Shailey: I honestly don't know what to believe. I don't believe she was pregnant when I gave her a massage. But that may be wishful thinking on my end because I hate to think I harmed her or her child in anyway! I don't like Todd (at all) and the only nice thing I can say about him is that he really loves his children. I believe he loves Trig.

Blade: Thanks so much for your time, Shailey. I'm sure the the readers of this blog will have questions so feel free to respond to them in the comments section.

This interview was conducted by Vickie Bottoms in the course of writing this book. The interview jumps right into the details of the beginning of the book when I first had sex with Todd Palin. This interview took place in September 2011.

Vickie: After the massage when Todd asked you to ride him how long was it before he contacted you again? What method of contact and what was said or done?

Shay: I don't think he did. He just came in about two months later in person and wanted to see me. As in get a massage. At this point I had seen Fred and one other person. I think this puts us at May of 2007. He did email me at the (redacted) email and let me know he was sending me a referral. I think I have one email stating such as well. Also I believe I saw him at least once at the poker games but again didn't really speak to him other than a hi.

Vickie: Did you see Todd in person again before he sent Fred to you? If so what happened?

Shay: Actually, no I don't think I did. I think about three weeks after he and I had sex, he sent Fred to me. He sent an email to the place I was working and generically said he was sending me a referral. He also said he was paying for the massage. The day after I massaged Fred, he came by the place and dropped off an envelope with money. It was $100.00. The women at worked teased me about it. I wasn't there when he had come by, so he must have either dropped it in the drop box or came in early that morning before 10:00 a.m.

Vickie: You stated that Fred wanted sex and he was mad that you didn't know. Was Fred's anger directed at you or Todd?

Shay: Fred was really angry with me, he thought I was playing coy and stupid. He called me a lot of derogatory names. That first time I didn't even give him a hand job. He was appeased in the end because I talked calmly to him even though he got irate. What happened was I had given him the intake form, and left the room for him to undress, then I went back in and he was completely naked standing by the massage table. I asked him to lie down and cover with a sheet and left the room. Then I came back and got lotion and he was dead quiet. I knew something wasn't quite right. I started to massage his back and the back of his legs. When I got to his feet he kept sighing and was restless. Not in a sexual way just in a bored way. He finally sat up and said was this all he was getting and I told him it was a full body massage (later I realized that was code for sex or happy endings), and he was like well are you going to take your top off or can we just have sex. And I was like WHAT???? And he told me Todd had told him that I would take care of him, they worked together on some projects and he didn't want to waste his time with a massage, and just wanted a good blow job. He worked himself up into quite a rage. Mad at Todd, but mostly at me for being so stupid and coy. It was quite an experience.

Vickie: Did you confront Todd about him sending you a

194

sex client without letting you know? If so was the confrontation in person or by phone or email. What did you say and what did Todd say?

Shay: I didn't get to confront him about it until he came in about two weeks later. I am not sure it was even a full two weeks. I did confront him. He smoothed it all over. Said it was his fault. His misunderstanding. That he just thinks I am so great and wanted to help me out. And I couldn't be a little girl anymore if I needed to make money. These people were somehow important and their needs important and needed someone who can understand that and not judge them. They had more to lose than me somehow, it was all very demeaning but yet sugary and in the moment it all seemed to make sense. He told me to advertise on Craigslist under Bonnie's, under beauty. He said he would start referring people to my add and even suggested I run and internet special. He let me know he would send me more clients and would pay me a little extra to cater to them. He told me I never had to have sex with anyone but a hand job would be a nice touch. He suggested I consider doing other things as well but never told me outright to do them. I wasn't happy and he could see that, he thought in the end the money would keep me in line and shut up. For a short time it did. He also wanted me to keep tabs on people, their names, when they came in, what they liked, etc.

Vickie: Spring of 2007 - Were you still working for the schools? Where were you doing the massages?

Shay: I worked as a sub until school let out in May or June. I think that year school let out in May. I also was continuing to grow my massage business, and started by word of mouth repairing people's computers.

Vickie: Around the fifth massage, Todd wanted to have sex with you. Were you surprised or did you have an idea that request was coming?

Shay: I tried to avoid him, get him to see someone else. He said he had to see me. I was happy when the massage seemed normal. I had already told him a few times I didn't like where it was going. That he was married anyway. But at the end of the massage he turned over and showed me how hard he was and pulled a condom out and asked me to "ride his cock" and he was a "bad boy" and I had to punish him. Then he was like oh you are so tight blah blah blah. He loved my "pussy" he wanted to taste it and all, you know do other stuff. He gave me $200.00 that time but after that it was always additional $50- $100. The less I moved or said anything the more he liked it. The more I said how sexy he was and how great his cock the more he enjoyed whatever he was doing. He really liked oral and he really liked to smell. I just would close my eyes and think of groceries or the kids or what we needed to get done the next day or whose calls did I need to return. I got zero pleasure from this. He didn't even try to make it good for me. That wasn't the point for him. I am sure he assumed I loved it. He isn't capable of thinking anything else.

Vickie: After you and Todd had sex, did he ever treat you like more than someone he was paying for sex? How did you feel about Todd at that point? Was he just a client, a friend with benefits or more?

Shay: No as we got more intimate it seems like he hated me or became more cold or business like. Because he spoke to me like he was a close friend it confused me, but I never felt loved or liked by him. He would ask me personal questions but never invited reciprocation. Thinking about all of it, YUCK. But looking back even though I didn't want to, he was so convincing, smooth, like what was the harm since we already did the other thing. Why would I hide such beautiful breast and deprive him and drive him crazy thinking about them and wasn't he handsome and was his penis normal was it too small, what did I think of him as a man....oh my god ...he was so insecure and whiny and needed constant reassurance.

Vickie: Let me know if I have this straight now for the time

196

when you first met Todd through the time when you and he had sex, your regular job was with the school system doing whatever they needed you to do. You also gave massages at the spa.

Shay: Correct, and I would babysit and do art projects on the side. Sometimes fix peoples computers. I was just doing anything I could to make money so I could provide clothes, foods, and pay the bills. I would make my massage schedule around the hours I wanted to work for the school. But the hours I worked I would have to be there at the spa. They would not call me in. Most of the time I gave massages early mornings before 10:00 a.m. and went to a sub job, got kids, dropped kids off at a sitter, or my parents, or extended daycare, and go back to spa and try to fit in a massage. Some days I didn't sub and just worked at the spa. It just depended on if I thought I could get clients.

Vickie: So when you did have appointments at the spa, was there an appointment book of some kind? Perhaps something you could see Todd Palin's name on?

Shay: Yes and the police have some of that. I may have copies and so does that spa. There is even an original intake form. I want to keep things as near to what really happened as possible.

Vickie: Exactly. When did you and Todd exchange email addresses?

Shay: Todd and I exchanged email addresses at the school when I first met him. I gave him a business card, Blue Hands was the name on it and the address for the mini spa I worked at.

Vickie: Okay let's fast forward in time to the Fall of 2009. By this time you had your own office space, you said Todd encouraged you to hook up with a business partner and her name was L.S. Can you tell me more about L.S.?

Shay: She really has a huge heart. She really wanted to make a life for her and her child. But by the week I saw how the drugs were consuming her, and her need to be on them, and her very drama intensive life. She talked loud, dressed loud, and loved to wear six inch heels. But she was adorable and fun!!! I would say she was infectious. Also she was someone who I could finally talk about the "trade" with and she shared her experiences with me, and we made loads of jokes. She also knew Todd Palin and what an asshole he was. She did not like him either. She blamed him for getting her addicted to drugs and to the life as we called it.

Vickie: You sound like you miss it a little. Do you miss being a prostitute?

Shay: I miss the money not the clients. I did get a rush doing some of the things I did. I like being safe even more.

Vickie: Okay, let me back track to right before you met L.S., the vacation you took was the trip to Ohio to meet Richard's family and while there he devastated you by announcing out of the blue in front of his family that he wasn't happy with your living arrangement?

Shay: Yes. After that trip we returned to Anchorage. We lived with him until June of 2010. But I strived to be more perfect, more attentive, and more attractive. The problem was clients thought I was doing it for them, Todd thought I was doing it for him. I was so stressed out. The original financial arrangement I had with Richard changed when we got back from Ohio, so when I started making more of my own money, Richard didn't ask questions. He just didn't want to be financially responsible,

Vickie: Okay... would you say that Todd paid you just enough to keep you hooked into the life but not enough to save up and be able to leave that lifestyle?

Shay: Yes! And he would bring little but expensive gifts from time to time, always with the promise that this would lead to an extremely rich life and I would be able to pay for my kids needs and get out of debt and finish school.

Vickie: So after Ohio your financial arrangements began to change with Richard. What is it you wanted from Richard exactly?

Shay: At first he did not expect me to help with daily expenses or living expenses. But after Ohio, he did want me to contribute. Part of the problem I think is his daughters perceived that I was using him in someway. I really wasn't, I loved him. I had hoped he would fall in love with me and then want to take care of me. In a way Richard kept me hooked too. I would say that Richard is slightly emotionally abusive when he doesn't get his way. Because even now he finds money for his expensive hobbies and wants. Richard lead a nice lifestyle. I do not begrudge him this, I just always wanted him to lift me up and give me love and support.

Vickie: Looking back at everything and having some distance from your life in Alaska, what decision have you come to about the sex trafficking...was Todd involved in that?

Shay: I would say yes.

Vickie: Were people actually sold as sex slaves?

Shay: That part I honestly do not know.

Vickie: Switching topics for a moment. Let's get back to Todd and Sarah. So Todd said that he and Sarah hadn't had sex in about two years. That could be interesting, considering the timing. If she was actually pregnant Todd might not even be the father.

Shay: Vickie it is times like this where I don't want this book. And I want to end this interview. I can't imagine how much people will hate me and how embarrassing it will be for me to see how completely stupid I was. In the moment when it was all happening it didn't feel like that. It felt like someone was acknowledging how hard my life was, how hard it was emotionally and financially. I had even told Todd once that every Christmas me and the kids always helped at a soup kitchen; do you know what they did the very next holiday? They volunteered at a soup kitchen. And made it seem like they always did that. That was me. The slimy bastard took my life and made it his and made my life vile. Well actually I let him do it to me but still. So to get back to your actual question, yes Todd had told me he and Sarah had not had sex in two years. However this is something men say all the time when they want sex from you.

Vickie: Shailey you have been through a lot. You have been very candid. After everything you have been through is there anything you want people to know?

Shay: I just want people to know how sorry I am for all of it. Not that I need their forgiveness but I am sorry. I live with what I did everyday. I hurt everyone who believed in me but mainly I hurt myself. I love my kids and all I ever wanted was to give them a great childhood. I never imagined I would have children much less children with special needs. For a long time I was very angry. That anger has now left me. I just want everyone to understand that life keeps happening. Just be more compassionate towards one another and always have a dream for yourself. You never know where life can take you or what doors can open up if you are brave enough to go through them.

Knowledge

Deep within my soul, there lies
a treasure greater than dreams...
Of Fascination
and
beyond imagination.
It is the key to within...
and beyond...
The key to everything.
We all possess this dear, dear thing.
The thing which we strive for.

© Shailey Lawes

APPENDICES

Timeline

2004

<u>February 05</u> My daughter, Salora was born. She was injured at birth resulting in life long disabilities

2005

<u>February 26</u> My son Brice was born. He was born five and half weeks early. He was born deaf and Autistic. Today he can hear.

2006

<u>November</u>   This is the month I first met Todd Palin.

<u>December 04</u> Sarah Palin took office as Governor of Alaska

<u>December 05</u> Todd Palin sent me an email telling me "you light up my life"

2007

<u>April 07</u> Shailey Tripp's baptism in the Church of Latter Day Saints

<u>April 20</u> My son had ear surgery. This enabled him to hear for the first time.

2008

March 11 My mom left for England due to her dad being ill

March 18 Maternal Grandfather died

March 21 Relief society dinner; I gave a speech on behalf
of Family Promise, as one of the board members

May 15   Great Uncle Bob passed away

May 17   Salora's big stage debut moment for dance

June 21   Eklutna Pow Wow, in which my whole family
participated. I also spoke and hosted a women's
circle

July 23   I put in a two week notice at All About You

August 06 My last day at All About You

December 08 I took a TSA test and passed

2009

January 02 Called TSA and found out my credit score
would not allow me to get the job

January 21 I gave a Family Promise talk, at Colony Middle
School

April 21-25 In Seattle for my daughter's surgery, 23rd was
the actual surgery

May 04 Attended network security event in Anchorage

May 8-9 Fairbanks, a trip I was asked to go on from Todd Palin

May 12 Salora check up in Seattle

May 13 My children graduated from pre-K & kindergarten

May 15-16 Seward, a trip I was asked to go on from Todd Palin

May 21-23 Atlanta, a trip I was asked to go on from Todd Palin

June 09 I saw and spoke with Todd Palin in Anchorage

June 12 Me and my children moved in with Richard in Anchorage

August 8 I had coffee with Todd Palin in Anchorage

August 11- 17 Anchorage trip for Todd Palin in which I had to tell my family members that I was leaving town to Atlanta

August 19 Signed lease for office space with Holly Wilson at Décor Lighting

October 01 Found out Salora is blind in one eye; she wears glasses for the first time

October 22-24 AFN, spoke at conference

2010

January 25, 2010 In the police reports of my arrest this is the day Laurie Jorgenson, Rachel Broady, and William Fortier phoned in a complaint to the police.

February 12-19 Trip for Todd to Huntsville, Al, Atlanta, GA, & Seattle, Wa and then back home. This trip was arranged by email, even though I was trying not to see him anymore. He gave my name and email out to other contacts of his and I was pressured into taking this trip

February 16, 2010 Wanda, a close personal friend of mine passed away from cancer.

March 1, 2010 Shaeffer Cox wife had him arrested in Fair banks

March 4, 2010 Kashawn Thomas arrested, Anchorage,

March 4, 2010 Shailey Tripp arrested, Anchorage

March 30, 2010 Wanda's memorial service. She was a close friend of mine and passed away from cancer on Feb. 16

May 13-21, 2010 Final trip for Todd Palin and Greg West to Huntsville, Al and Seattle, WA. Once I saw the extent of the operation and that some military personel were involved I got scared and was done.

June 01 I had court for my March 4 arrest

June 11 I had another court appearance

June 15 Court

June 16 Court

June 16 Moved to another state

December 15 The National Enquirer notified the Palins about a mistress/prostitution story

2011

January 19   The National Enquirer runs a story saying that Todd Palin is caught in a sleazy sex scandal

January 25 The Anchorage Police Department issues their press release to the National Enquirer thus the Enquirer puts this new information regarding the APD on their website

January 26 The National Enquirer runs a second story about Shailey Tripp giving Sarah Palin a massage

January 27 Sarah Palin announced on the Bob and Mark show and states that her husband has nothing to do with a prostitution ring in Anchorage.

The Police Reports

I have included a copy of the police reports dated March, 4, 2010. This is the date of my arrest. The significance of the police reports are varied but two main points are made by showing these police reports. The first important point is that the information these police reports contain directly contradict the press release Lt. Dave Parker submitted to the National Enquirer in January of 2011. Secondly, the police reports demonstrate there were a lot of inconsistencies in each report and show that clearly three people phoned in a complaint to the police. Their complaint was of loud noises that sounded like sexual behavior and men coming in and out of the building, and specifically Todd Palin coming in and out of the building, which supposedly led to these people making a complaint of prostitution to the local police.

ANCHORAGE POLICE DEPARTMENT

10-3948

4501 ELMORE RD

ALASKA 99507
Nature of Call
PROSTITUTE

907-786-8600

Reported Date
01/24/2010

Officer
LEE, BRENDAN

Administrative Information

Agency				Report No	Supplement No	Reported Date	Reported Time	CAD Call No
ANCHORAGE POLICE DEPARTMENT				10-3948	0002	01/24/2010	10:13	100240322
Status	Nature of Call							
REPORT	PROSTITUTION		JDN360					
Location					City		ZIP Code	Rep Dist
1601 ABBOTT RD #204					ANC		99507	26K1
Area	Beat	Officer				Assignment		Entered by
3	42	29597/LEE, BRENDAN				DETECTIVES VICE		29597
Assignment		Confidential	RMS Transfer	Approving Official		Approval Date		
DETECTIVES VICE		VICE	Pending	29597		03/04/2010		
Approval Time								
17:14:35								

Narrative

INFORMATION

On March 4, 2010 at 1237 hours, I attended a briefing by Officer NOLDER reference a massage parlor sting that would take place at 1300 at 1601 Abbott Rd. I was tasked with surveillance of the east side of the target location. At 1259, I arrived and I parked on the east side of the building in the parking lot of a hardware store. At 1301 hours, Officer NOLDER went into the building on the west side of the building. At 1315 hours, I heard Officer NOLDER say the code statement for us to come in and arrest the female. I pulled around the building and as I was pulling up, the other Detectives had already gone in and detained the female. I observed the office to have a desk, and in the back room, there was a table with a sheet and blanket on it. The lights were turned down low.

CASE STATUS: CLOSED BY ARREST

Report Officer	Printed At	
29597/LEE, BRENDAN	03/05/2010 15:16	Page 1 of 1

ANCHORAGE POLICE DEPARTMENT

4501 ELMORE RD

ALASKA 99507

Nature of Call
PROSTITUTE

907-786-8600

Reported Date
01/24/2010

Officer
BURNS, DAVID

Administrative Information

Agency		Report No	Supplement No	Reported Date	Reported Time	CAD Call No
ANCHORAGE POLICE DEPARTMENT		10-3948	0004	01/24/2010	10:13	100240322

Status	Nature of Call					
REPORT	PROSTITUTION		XMN360			

Location			City		ZIP Code	Rep Dist
1601 ABBOTT RD #204			ANC		99507	26E1

Area	Beat	Officer			Assignment	Entered by
S	42	30356/BURNS, DAVID			DETECTIVES VICE	30356

Assignment	Confidential	RMS Transfer	Approving Officer	Approval Date	
DETECTIVES VICE	VICE	Pending	30356	03/04/2010	

Approval Time					
20:15:04					

Narrative

INFORMATION:
On 3/4/2010 at about 1300 hours the Vice Unit conducted a massage parlor operation.

At about 1237 hours I attended a briefing by Officer NOLDER and Det. MCKINNON. Det. MCKINNON advised that he received a tip reference a possible prostitution operation at 1601 Abbott Road #202 (S&L Associates).

Officer NOLDER advised that he called 861-1869 to make an appointment with "Tia". Officer NOLDER got the phone number from a listing on Craig's List in the adult services location. After several phone calls Officer NOLDER arranged a massage with "TIA" at 1300 hours.

ACTION TAKEN:
For this operation I was assigned to keep the log and be part of the entry team. At about 1259 hours Officer NOLDER arrived on scene and entered the building. At about 1315 hours I heard Officer NOLDER say the take down phrase over the safety wire.

OBSERVATIONS:
When I entered suite #202 I observed Officer NOLDER standing an office area with a black female adult (KASHAWN THOMAS). I assisted other vice units in clearing the suite and securing the buisness.

ACTION TAKEN:
Once the business was secured I went to apply for and was granted a search warrant by Judge SWIDERSKI for 1601 Abbott Suite #202 (10-390). At about 1531 hours I arrived at 1601 Abbott Suite #202 and served the warrant with several other vice officers.

INFORMATION:
Several items were seized during the search of the business. To include office documents, computers, office machines, unused condoms, used condoms, calendars and books with client phone numbers in them.
Several photographs were taken during the search and after. I left a copy of the search warrant and the affidavit on scene. While I was applying for the search warrant the business owner "Tia" arrived on scene. "Tia" and THOMAS were arrested, processed and remanded to ANJ after a bail hearing.

CASE STATUS: Pending

Report Officer	Printed At	
30356/BURNS, DAVID	03/05/2010 15:16	Page 1 of 1

ANCHORAGE POLICE DEPARTMENT

4501 ELMORE RD

ALASKA 99507

Nature of Call
PROSTITUTE

907-786-8600

Reported Date
01/24/2010

Officer
NEER, DAWN

Administrative Information

Agency	Report No	Supplement No	Reported Date	Reported Time	CAD Call No
ANCHORAGE POLICE DEPARTMENT	10-3948	0006	01/24/2010	10:13	100240322

Status	Nature of Call				
REPORT	PROSTITUTION	XMN360			

Location		City	ZIP Code	Rep Dist
1601 ABBOTT RD #204		ANC	99507	25E1

Area	Beat	Officer		Assignment	Entered By
S	42	1459/NEER,DAWN		DETECTIVES VICE	1459

Assignment	RMS Transfer	Approving Officer	Approval Date	Approval Time
DETECTIVES VICE	Pending	1459	03/05/2010	15:57:30

Narrative

INFORMATION

On 3-4-2010 at about 1237 hrs I attended a briefing held by Det. MCKINNON. Det. MCKINNON told us that Officer NOLDER was going to pose as an undercover John and attempt to get a deal for prostitution at 1601 Abbott Rd #202. Det. MCKINNON had gotten information that this location is a massage parlor that is also practicing prostitution.

At about 1259 hrs I watched Officer NOLDER enter the common entry of the business. At about 1315 hrs we made entry into the business after Officer NOLDER advised us to come inside and the deal had been made. When I entered, I saw a black female later identified as KASHAWN THOMAS was inside the business. I put her into handcuffs and sat her down in a chair in the office area. The rest of the unit cleared the business and nobody else was found to be inside. I left with Officer BURNS and BUSHJE and returned to APD in order to write the search warrant for the business. Officer BURNS wrote the affidavit for the search warrant and also applied for the warrant.

I assisted in the search of the business and also was tasked with evidence custodian. I found $80 in buy money in the top left drawer of the desk in the office area. I packaged all evidence seized and put it into property and evidence when we returned to APD. I left a copy of all property and evidence forms at the business when we left. Officer NOLDER secured the business upon our exit.

CASE STATUS: CLOSED

Report Officer
1459/NEER,DAWN

Printed At
03/05/2010 21:47

Page 1 of 1

213

ANCHORAGE POLICE DEPARTMENT

10-3948

Supplement No
0006

4501 ELMORE RD

ALASKA 99507
Nature of Call
PROSTITUTE

907-786-8600

Reported Date
01/24/2010

Officer
NEER, DAWN

Administrative Information

Agency		Report No	Supplement No	Reported Date	Reported Time	CAD Call No
ANCHORAGE POLICE DEPARTMENT		10-3948	0006	01/24/2010	10:13	100240322

Status	Nature of Call					
REPORT	PROSTITUTION	XMN360				

Location				City	ZIP Code	Rep Dist
1601 ABBOTT RD #204				ANC	99507	26E1

Area	Beat	Officer			Assignment	Entered by
S	42	1459/NEER, DAWN			DETECTIVES VICE	1459

Assignment	R&B Transfer	Approving Officer	Approval Date	Approval Time
DETECTIVES VICE	Pending	1459	03/05/2010	16:57:38

Narrative
INFORMATION

On 3-4-2010 at about 1237 hrs I attended a brieifing held by Det. MCKINNON. Det. MCKINNON told us that Officer NOLDER was going to pose as an undercover John and attempt to get a deal for prostitution at 1601 Abbott Rd #202. Det. MCKINNON had gotten information that this location is a massage parlor that is also practicing prostitution.

At about 1259 hrs I watched Officer NOLDER enter the common entry of the business. At about 1315 hrs we made entry into the business after Officer NOLDER advsied us to come inside and the deal had been made. When I entered, I saw a black female later identified as KASHAWN THOMAS was inside the business. I put her into handcuffs and sat her down in a chair in the office area. The rest of the unit cleared the business and nobody else was found to be inside. I left with Officer BURNS and BUSHUE and returned to APD in order to write the search warrant for the business. Officer BURNS wrote the affidavit for the search warrant and also applied for the warrant.

I assisted in the search of the business and also was tasked with evidence custodian. I found $80 in buy money in the top left drawer of the desk in the office rarea. I packaged all evidence seized and put it into property and evidence when we returned to APD. I left a copy of all property and evidence forms at the business when we left. Officer NOLDER secured the business upon our exit.

CASE STATUS: CLOSED

Report Officer
1459/NEER, DAWN

Printed At
03/05/2010 21:47

Page 1 of 1

ANCHORAGE POLICE DEPARTMENT

4501 ELMORE RD

ALASKA 99507
Nature of Call
PROSTITUTE

907-786-8600

Reported Date
01/24/2010

Officer
NOLDER, JOSHUA R

Administrative Information

Agency				Report No	Supplement No	Reported Date	Reported Time	CAD Call No
ANCHORAGE POLICE DEPARTMENT				10-3948	0001	01/24/2010	10:13	100240322
Status	Nature of Call							
REPORT	PROSTITUTION			XMN360				
Location					City		ZIP Code	Rep Dist
1601 ABBOTT RD #204					ANC		99507	26E1
Area	Beat	Officer						Entered by
S	42	28528/NOLDER, JOSHUA R				Assignment		28528
						DETECTIVES VICE		
Assignment		Confidential	RMS Transfer	Approving Officer		Approval Date		
DETECTIVES VICE		VICE	Pending	28528		03/04/2010		
Approval Time								
19:20:20								

Narrative

INFORMATION:

On 3/4/2010, at approx. 0758 hours I attempted to contact "Tia" reference a Craigslist ad for "Tia's Massage" at 891-1869. There was no answer and I left a message about wanting to schedule a massage for 1300 hours. A few minutes later I received a text message from phone number 775-3235 stating: "Sorry I missed u. Call bak after 9:30". I replied "ok" to the text message.

At approx. 1002 hours I called the 775-3235 number and spoke with a female. I asked the female if she was "Tia" and she said she was. I asked if I could schedule a one hour massage for 1300 hours and she said that would be "no problem". I asked "Tia" where she was located and she said the business was located at 1601 Abbott suite # 202 and the door said "C.S." on it.

At approx. 1237 hours Det. Mckinnon and I briefed the Vice unit about attempting to arrest "Tia" for prostitution if sex for money was arranged. At approx. 1254 hours I arrived at 1601 Abbott.

At approx. 1301 hours I entered the office door which is on the second floor facing south. A young black female later identified as KASHAWN THOMAS greeted me, I told her I was there for a massage appointment. The female told me to follow her and showed me to a room to the northeast in the very small office. I asked THOMAS if she was "Tia", THOMAS replied she was not. THOMAS asked if I wanted to wait for "Tia" or get a massage from her. I replied that I would be fine with a massage from THOMAS.

At approx. 1303 hours THOMAS asked what kind of massage did I want and I told her an hour. THOMAS asked if I wanted a whole hour of massage or an hour with a massage. I replied that I wanted an hour with a massage and THOMAS said that would be $210. THOMAS directed me to get prepared and lay down on the table while she exited the room with the $220 I had handed her. I laid down on the table on my stomach with a blanket covering my mid-section.

THOMAS re-entered the room and asked what type of massaged did I want. I asked what kind of massages where there. THOMAS replied that there was a usual massage, a "deep tissue" massage and a "sensual massage". I told THOMAS that I wanted a "sensual massage" THOMAS began rubbing my back with oil. A few minutes into the massage THOMAS asked I wanted my legs massaged as well and I replied that I did. THOMAS said she would return but had to lock the door to the business. THOMAS returned and removed the blanket from my mid-section and began massaging my legs.

At approx. 10 minutes into the massage THOMAS told me to turn onto my back. THOMAS asked me if I knew what was entailed in a "sensual massage". I replied to THOMAS that I did not. THOMAS motioned her left hand

Report Officer	Printed At	
28528/NOLDER, JOSHUA R	03/04/2010 19:21	Page 1 of 2

215

ANCHORAGE POLICE DEPARTMENT

Narrative

in a closed formation up and down which I recognized as manual ejaculation and said it was included for $210. I asked how much "the full experience" was and she replied "the full experience, that's $250".

THOMAS directed me to get the additional money while she began undressing. I got up from the massage table and retrieved the cash. I handed the cash to THOMAS and asked her if she heard a car alarm. THOMAS turned off the radio in the room and said she would go and check if I liked. I wrapped myself in a blanket and walked from the room to the front of the office. I unlocked the front door and at approx 1315 hours the other members of the Vice unit entered. THOMAS was placed under arrest.

At approx. 1345 hours "Tia" or SHAILEY TRIPP as she would be identified later entered the business and was contacted by Det. McKinnon. TRIPP was placed under arrest for maintaining a place of prostitution.

INTERVIEW WITH KASHAWN THOMAS: NOT RECORDED (MALFUNCTION)
At approx. 1500 hours I read THOMAS her Miranda rights which she waived. THOMAS said she had been working at the massage parlor for approx. two months and in that time she has performed approx. 13 sexual acts, mostly oral copulation, but also manual ejaculation and full sexual intercourse. THOMAS said the business provides an approximate 50% mix of actual massages and sexual acts. THOMAS said she had intended to just provide massages but the owner SHAILEY TRIPP who she knows as "Tia" told THOMAS that if she wanted to make more money and have return customers she would have to provide sexual favors for money. THOMAS said she needed the money as she is six and a half weeks pregnant.

ACTION TAKEN:
THOMAS was released on her own recognizance with all appropriate court paperwork due to her lack of criminal convictions and pregnant status.

INFORMATION:
At approx. 1531 hours Ofc. Burns arrived with a search warrant (10-390sw)he had received for the business. I searched the massage room (north east of business) where I found Astroglide and KY Jelly (both photographed). I also found a used condom and condom wrapper in a small trash basket underneath the table the Astroglide and other oils were located.

In the office area I seized a Sony laptop and credit card machine as well as various office paperwork such as client lists and expense report. All property was seized as evidence and submitted as such. Det. Neer also assisted with the search and was the evidence custodian.

CASE STATUS:
Closed

ANCHORAGE POLICE DEPARTMENT

4501 ELMORE RD

ALASKA 99507
Nature of Call
PROSTITUTE

Reported Date
01/24/2010

Officer
MCKINNON, JOHN

907-786-8600

Administrative Information

Agency				Report No	Supplement No	Reported Date	Reported Time	CAD Call No
ANCHORAGE POLICE DEPARTMENT				10-3948	0003	01/24/2010	10:13	100240322
Status	Nature of Call							
REPORT	PROSTITUTION			XMN360				
Location					City	Zip Code		Reg Dist
1601 ABBOTT RD #202					ANC	99507		26E1
Area	Beat	Officer				Assigned		Printed by
S	42	1456/MCKINNON, JOHN				DETECTIVES VICE		1456
Assignment		Confidential	RMS Transfer	Approving Officer		Approval Date		
DETECTIVES VICE		VICE	Pending	1456		03/04/2010		
Approval Time								
20:29:42								

WITNESS 1: BROADY, RACHEL

Involvement	Invl No	Type		Name			MNI	Race
WITNESS	1	Individual		BROADY, RACHEL			662733	White
Sex	DOB	Age	Juvenile?					
Female	05/08/1974	35	No					
Type		ID No				OLS		
Operator License		7020346				Alaska		
Phone Type	Phone No			Date				
Business	(907)522-7350			01/24/2010				

WITNESS 2: JORGENSON, LAURIE

Involvement	Invl No	Type		Name			MNI	Race
WITNESS	2	Individual		JORGENSON, LAURIE			383918	White
Sex	DOB	Age	Juvenile?	Height	Weight	Hair Color		Eye Color
Female	12/04/1961	48	No	5'03"	125#	Blond or Strawberry		Blue
Type		ID No				OLS		
Operator License		7162963				Alaska		
Social Security Number		518-84-1433						
Phone Type	Phone No			Date				
Business	(907)349-4123			01/24/2010				

Narrative

SYNOPSIS: On 3/4/2010, I arrested Shailey TRIPP for one count of maintaining a place of prostitution. Ofc Nolder arrested Kashawn THOMAS for one count of practicing prostitution. THOMAS was cited and released under citation A1425341. Ofc Burns applied for and was granted search warrant 10-390sw. A telephonic bail hearing was conducted with Magistrate Clark and bail was set at $5000 c/c. No area restrictions. TRIPP was remanded to ANJ without incident.

INFORMATION: On or about 2/1/2010, I was assigned this case for investigative follow-up by Sgt Padgett.

ACTIONS TAKEN: I reviewed the case filed by Ofc Billet and determined solvability based on the information given. I reviewed the following adult websites and determined the phone number TRIPP provided on her lease agreement with G&H Properties was the same as the postings: backpage.com and Craig's List.org (see postings)

INFORMATION: The most recent posting which was posted on Craig's List was dated 3/1/2010 at 2:43pm. The phone number listed was 891-1869 and asked the respondent to contact TIA (believed to be TRIPP). Ofc Nolder made contact at this number and received a text message back from 775-3235, this is the number TRIPP had on

Report Officer	Printed At	
1456/MCKINNON, JOHN	03/05/2010 15:16	Page 1 of 2

ANCHORAGE POLICE DEPARTMENT

Narrative

her rental agreement for the office space. When TRIPP was taken into custody, she had the phone with the 775-3235 number. This same number was on the door emblem of suite 202 (see photos) where the act of prostitution took place.

EVIDENCE SEIZED: See P&E.

CASE STATUS: Closed by arrest.

ANCHORAGE POLICE DEPARTMENT

4501 ELMORE RD

ALASKA 99507
Nature of Call
PROSTITUTE

907-786-8600

Reported Date
01/24/2010

Officer
MCKINNON, JOHN

Administrative Information

Agency			Report No	Supplement No	Reported Date		Reported Time	CAD Call No
ANCHORAGE POLICE DEPARTMENT			10-3948	0003	01/24/2010		10:13	100240322
Status	Nature of Call							
REPORT	PROSTITUTION			XMN360				
Location					City		ZIP Code	Rep Dist
1601 ABBOTT RD #202					ANC		99507	26E1
Area	Beat	Officer				Assignment		Entered by	
S	42	1456/MCKINNON, JOHN				DETECTIVES VICE		1456	
Assignment		Confidential	RMS Transfer	Approving Officer		Approval Date			
DETECTIVES VICE		VICE	Pending	1456		03/04/2010			
Approval Time									
20:29:42									

WITNESS 1: BROADY, RACHEL

Involvement	Invl No	Type		Name			MNI	Race
WITNESS	1	Individual		BROADY, RACHEL			662733	White
Sex	DOB		Age	Juvenile?				
Female	05/08/1974		35	No				
Type			ID No			OLS		
Operator License			7020346			Alaska		
Phone Type	Phone No			Date				
Business	(907)522-7350			01/24/2010				

WITNESS 2: JORGENSON, LAURIE

Involvement	Invl No	Type		Name				MNI	Race
WITNESS	2	Individual		JORGENSON, LAURIE				383918	White
Sex	DOB		Age	Juvenile?	Height	Weight	Hair Color		Eye Color
Female	12/04/1961		48	No	5'03"	125#	Blond or Strawberry		Blue
Type			ID No			OLS			
Operator License			7162963			Alaska			
Type			ID No						
Social Security Number			518-84-1433						
Phone Type	Phone No			Date					
Business	(907)349-4123			01/24/2010					

Narrative

SYNOPSIS: On 3/4/2010, I arrested Shailey TRIPP for one count of maintaining a place of prostitution. Ofc Nolder arrested Kashawn THOMAS for one count of practicing prostitution. THOMAS was cited and released under citation A1425341. Ofc Burns applied for and was granted search warrant 10-390sw. A telephonic bail hearing was conducted with Magistrate Clark and bail was set at $5000 c/c. No area restrictions. TRIPP was remanded to ANJ without incident.

INFORMATION: On or about 2/1/2010, I was assigned this case for investigative follow-up by Sgt Padgett.

ACTIONS TAKEN: I reviewed the case filed by Ofc Billet and determined solvability based on the information given. I reviewed the following adult websites and determined the phone number TRIPP provided on her lease agreement with G&H Properties was the same as the postings: backpage.com and Craig's List.org (see postings)

INFORMATION: The most recent posting which was posted on Craig's List was dated 3/1/2010 at 2:43pm. The phone number listed was 891-1869 and asked the respondent to contact TIA (believed to be TRIPP). Ofc Nolder made contact at this number and received a text message back from 775-3235; this is the number TRIPP had on

Report Officer	Printed At	
1456/MCKINNON, JOHN	03/05/2010 15:16	Page 1 of 2

ANCHORAGE POLICE DEPARTMENT

10-3948

Supplement No
0001

4501 ELMORE RD

ALASKA 99507
Nature of Call
PROSTITUTE

Reported Date
01/24/2010

Officer
NOLDER, JOSHUA

907-786-8600

Administrative Information

Agency ANCHORAGE POLICE DEPARTMENT			Report No 10-3948	Supplement No 0001	Reported Date 01/24/2010	Reported Time 10:33	CAD Call No 10C240522
Status REPORT	Nature of Call PROSTITUTION			ZMN360			
Location 1601 ABBOTT RD #204				City ANC		Zip Code 99507	Rpt Dist 26E1
Area B	Dist 42	Officer 28528/NOLDER, JOSHUA			Assignment DETECTIVES VICE		Entered by 28528
Assignment DETECTIVES VICE		Confidential VICE	RMS Transfer Pending	Approving Officer 28528	Approval Date 03/04/2010		
Approval Time 19:20:20							

Narrative

INFORMATION:

On 3/4/2010, at approx. 0755 hours I attempted to contact "Tia" reference a Craigslist ad for "Tia's Massage" at 891-1869. There was no answer and I left a message about wanting to schedule a massage for 1300 hours. A few minutes later I received a text message from phone number 775-3235 stating: "Sorry I missed u. Call bak after 9:30". I replied "ok" to the text message.

At approx. 1002 hours I called the 775-3235 number and spoke with a female. I asked the female if she was "Tia" and she said she was. I asked if I could schedule a one hour massage for 1300 hours and she said that would be "no problem". I asked "Tia" where she was located and she said the business was located at 1601 Abbott suite # 202 and the door said "C.S." on it.

At approx. 1237 hours Det. McKinnon and I briefed the Vice unit about attempting to arrest "Tia" for prostitution if sex for money was arranged. At approx. 1254 hours I arrived at 1601 Abbott.

At approx. 1301 hours I entered the office door which is on the second floor facing south. A young black female later identified as KASHAWN THOMAS greeted me, I told her I was there for a massage appointment. The female told me to follow her and showed me to a room to the northeast in the very small office. I asked THOMAS if she was "Tia", THOMAS replied she was not. THOMAS asked if I wanted to wait for "Tia" or get a massage from her. I replied that I would be fine with a massage from THOMAS.

At approx. 1303 hours THOMAS asked what kind of massage did I want and I told her an hour. THOMAS asked if I wanted a whole hour of massage or an hour with a massage. I replied that I wanted an hour with a massage and THOMAS said that would be $210. THOMAS directed me to get prepared and lay down on the table while she exited the room with the $220 I had handed her. I laid down on the table on my stomach with a blanket covering my mid-section.

THOMAS re-entered the room and asked what type of massage did I want. I asked what kind of massages where there. THOMAS replied that there was a usual massage, a "deep tissue" massage and a "sensual massage". I told THOMAS that I wanted a "sensual massage" THOMAS began rubbing my back with oil. A few minutes into the massage THOMAS asked I wanted my legs massaged as well and I replied that I did. THOMAS said she would return but had to lock the door to the business. THOMAS returned and removed the blanket from my mid-section and began massaging my legs.

At approx. 10 minutes into the massage THOMAS told me to turn onto my back. THOMAS asked me if I knew what was entailed in a "sensual massage". I replied to THOMAS that I did not. THOMAS motioned her left hand

Report Officer 28528/NOLDER, JOSHUA	Printed At 03/05/2010 15:16	Page 1 of 2

220

IN THE DISTRICT/SUPERIOR COURT FOR THE STATE OF ALASKA
AT ___ANCHORAGE___

| SEARCH WARRANT |
| NO. _____ SW |

Relates to case number(s):

___10-3948___

_____

TO: Any Peace Officer

Having received information under oath from ___OFFICER DAVID BURNS___

_____

given ☐ in person   ☐ by telephone   ☒ by original affidavit   ☐ by faxed affidavit

I find probable cause to believe that

☐   on the person of _____

☒   on the premises known as ___1601 ABBOTT RD, SUITE #202___
___ANCHORAGE, ALASKA. SUITE #202 DOOR ON 2ND___
___FLOOR WITH SIGN FOR SAL ASSOC, 375-3235___
_____ at ___ANCHORAGE, ALASKA___
                                      (city and state)

there is now being concealed property, namely:

SEE ATTACHMENT "A"

Page 1 of 4
CR-706 (8/08)(st.4)
SEARCH WARRANT

AS 12.35.010-.120
Crim. R. 37

221

and that such property (see AS 12.35.020)

☒ 1. is evidence of the particular crime(s) of _Vachune Ashburn_
and prohibited thrust Absinthe.

☐ 2. tends to show that _____
committed the particular crime(s) of _____
_____.

☐ 3. is stolen or embezzled property.

☐ 4. was used as a means of committing a crime.

☐ 5. is in the possession of a person who intends to use it as a means of committing a crime.

☐ 6. is one of the above types of property and is in the possession of
_____, to whom
_____ delivered it to conceal it.

☐ 7. is evidence of health and safety violations.

YOU ARE HEREBY COMMANDED to search the person or premises named for the property specified, serving this warrant, and if the property be found there, to seize it, holding it secure pending further order of the court, leaving a copy of this warrant, and all supporting affidavits, and a receipt of property taken. You shall also prepare a written inventory of any property seized as a result of the search pursuant to or in conjunction with the warrant. You shall make the inventory in the presence of the applicant for the warrant and the person from whose possession or premises the property is taken, if they are present, or in the presence of at least one credible person other than the warrant applicant or person from whose possession or premises said property is taken. You shall sign the inventory and return it and the warrant within 30 days after this date to this court as required by law.

YOU SHALL SERVE THIS WARRANT:

☑ between the hours of 7:00 a.m. and 10:00 p.m.

☐ between the hours of _____ ☐ a.m. ☐ p.m.

and _____ ☐ a.m. ☐ p.m.

☐ at any time of the day or night.

Page 2 of 4
CR-706 (8/08)(st.4)
SEARCH WARRANT

AS 12.35.010-.120
Crim. R. 37

222

SEARCH WARRANT NO. _____ SW

YOU SHALL MAKE THE SEARCH:

☒ immediately.
☐ within _____ ☐ days ☐ hours.
☐ within 10 days.
☐ contingent upon the happening of the events expected to occur as set forth in the supporting testimony, specifically _____

_____

_____

From the information provided in the application for the warrant, I find compelling reasons to postpone delivery of this notice beyond the time set in Criminal Rule 37(b).[1] Therefore, this notice must be given:

☒ immediately upon seizure of the property.
☐ within a reasonable period, not to exceed 90 days from this date.
☐ within _____ days, which I have determined to be a reasonable time in this case.

If you cannot deliver the notice within this time limit, you must apply to the court for an extension of the time limit. Your sworn application must show good cause for the extension.

(SEAL)

_____   _____
            Date   Judge/Magistrate

_____ ☐ a.m. ☒ p.m.   _____
      Time Issued   Type or Print Name

TELEPHONIC SEARCH WARRANTS. If this search warrant was issued by telephone, the judicial officer named above has orally authorized the applicant for this warrant to sign the judicial officer's name. AS 12.35.015(d).

Time Warrant Served: _____

---

[1] *Jones v. State*, 646 P.2d 243, 249 (Alaska App. 1982). Reasons for postponement include, but are not limited to: avoiding jeopardizing a confidential informant's safety, avoiding impairing the informant's investigative efforts in other cases, and allowing time for follow-up investigations in this case.

Page 3 of 4
CR-706 (6/07)(st.4)
SEARCH WARRANT

AS 12.35.010-.120
Crim. R. 37

223

SEARCH WARRANT NO. _____SW

RECEIPT AND INVENTORY OF PROPERTY SEIZED
(Continued)

_____
_____
_____
_____
_____
_____
_____
_____
_____

RETURN

I received the attached search warrant on _____, 20_____, and have executed it as follows:

On _____, 20___, at ____ a.m./p.m., I searched ☐ the person ☒ the premises described in the warrant, and I left a copy of the warrant ☐ with ☐ at _____.
(person warrant was left with or place warrant was left)

The above inventory of property taken pursuant to the warrant was made in the presence of _____ and of _____.

I swear that this inventory is a true and detailed account of all property taken by me on the authority of this warrant.

_____
Name and Title

Signed and sworn to before me on _____, 20___.

(SEAL)

_____
Judge/Magistrate

_____
Type or Print Name

Page 4 of 4
CR-706 (5/06)(st.4)
SEARCH WARRANT

AS 12.35.010-.120
Crim. R. 37

224

IN THE DISTRICT COURT FOR
THE STATE OF ALASKA

FILED in the Trial Courts
State of Alaska Third District

MAR 4 2010

Clerk of the Courts
By_____ Deputy

THIRD JUDICIAL DISTRICT

IN THE MATTER OF)
SEARCH WARRANT)
AUTHORIZATION)
3AN 10- 390   SW)

DAVID BURNS
AFFIDAVIT OF ▓▓▓▓▓▓▓

STATE OF ALASKA)
) ss.
THIRD JUDICIAL DISTRICT)

Certification

I certify that:

___X___ This document and its attachments do not contain information that is confidential under AS 12.61.110 or the name of a victim of a crime listed in AS 12.61.140.

_____ This document or an attachment contains confidential information that may be placed in a court file under an exception listed in AS 12.61.130(b). This information appears at paragraph _____. This document and its attachments do not contain the name of a victim of a crime listed in AS 12.61.140.

I, David Burns, being first duly sworn upon oath, depose and state as follows:

1. I am a Police Officer employed by the Municipality of Anchorage Police Department and am presently assigned to the Anchorage Police Department's Detective Division in the Vice Unit. This assignment includes investigation of cases related to prostitution, human trafficking and controlled substances.

1

225

2. I have been employed with the Anchorage Police Department for over four (4) years. During this time I have completed a twenty six (26) week training academy, 72 day FTO process, assigned to the Uniformed Patrol Division Mid Shift Patrol, and now the Vice Unit.

3. I attended and graduated from a five month police academy operated by APD. While attending APD's academy, I received training and instruction on devices, paraphernalia, techniques, and practices used by people engaged in the use, possession, manufacture, and trafficking of controlled substances. In an extension of APD's academy, and subsequent to graduation from APD's academy, I received training and instruction from several APD field training officers. This training included investigation of crimes involving the use, possession, manufacture, and trafficking of controlled substances in the Anchorage area.

4. During the course of my various assignments, I have investigated both misdemeanor and felony crimes. I have applied for and received a multitude of arrest and search warrants. I also have served and assisted in the serving of numerous arrest and search warrants.

5. Prior to being employed by APD I was a Firefighter Paramedic. During that time I received training in anatomy physiology, pharmacology, drug administration, drug laws, hazardous materials, and firefighting techniques.

6. I attended training from the ATF on firearms, interview techniques, and hidden car compartments. I also have attended several in-service trainings on DUI investigation / enforcement, search-seizure and DRE investigations.

2

7. The majority of my police experience has been assigned to uniform patrol on the midnight shift. My duties include watching for illegal activities, interviewing witnesses, victims and suspects, developing probable cause for cases, examining crime scenes in order to develop evidence to substantiate or disprove the allegation being investigated, handling and processing various types of evidence, utilizing human sources of information to resolve drug and other criminal related investigations, and assembling cases for possible prosecution by State and Municipal Offices. In my law enforcement career, I have conducted drug related investigations, involving the use, possession, manufacture, and trafficking of marijuana, lysergic acid diethylamide (LSD) cocaine hydrochloride, cocaine base (crack), heroin, ecstasy (MDMA), methamphetamine, controlled prescription medication While conducting these investigations, I have interviewed several people, involved either directly or indirectly with the crimes being investigated. I have also served or assisted in serving several drug related search warrants resulting in the seizure of the above mentioned drugs as well as firearms, ammunition, packaging materials, assorted concealment containers, cutting agents, digital and beam scales, cellular telephones, pagers, surveillance systems, marijuana grow operations, methamphetamine laboratories, cameras, body armor, memory cards, computers and related equipment, documents, money, precious metals, gems, stolen property, address books, and assorted paraphernalia utilized to ingest controlled substances.

8. During my time in the Vice unit I have participated in prostitution operations, to include the investigation of Massage parlors.

9. The information in this affidavit is based on the Affiant's personal knowledge and/or the observations of other officers involved in this investigation as reported to me either orally or via their written reports. This investigation concerns Practicing Prostitution in any degree.

FACTS AND CIRCUMSTANCES FOR APD CASE #10-3948

10. On 1/24/2010 WILLIAM FORTIER contacted APD Officer BILLIET to report possible prostitution activity of one of the tenants the building. The building is located at 1601 Abbott and the tenant resides in suite #202. FORTIER told Officer BILLIET he rented #202 to SHAILEY TRIPP who said she was using the space for computer based business.

3

11. FORTIER reported that he started to observe that most of the business going into suite at was at night. FORTIER also noted ravens pulled used condoms from the dumpster of the business. After that he took notice of a large amount of used condoms and condom wrappers in the trash.

12. FORTIER showed Officer BILLIET the sign on Suite #202 and it read "S&L Associates". The phone number on the door was 775-5165. FORTIER provided the rental agreement with TRIPP. The phone listed for TRIPP on the agreement was 775-3235.

13. On 3/4/2010 Officer NOLDER called "TIA" at 891-1869 (from a posting on Craig's List adult services posting number 162-3874463) and left a message. Later in the morning "TIA" text Officer NOLDER from 775-3235 and told him to call back after 0930 hours. At 1000 hours Officer NOLDR contacted "TIA" (calling 775-3235) and arranged to meet at 1300 hours at 1601 Abbott Road Suite #202.

14. At about 1301 hours Officer NOLDER entered S&L Associates at 1601 Abbot Suite #202. He was met by a black female adult (KASHAWN THOMAS). Officer NOLDER told THOMAS that he had an appointment at 1300 hours with "TIA". THOMAS told Officer NOLDER that "TIA" was not there and asked how long he wanted. Officer NOLDER arranged to pay 210.00 dollars for an hour long massage.

15. Once the massage started THOMAS asked Officer NOLDER what type he wanted. THOMAS advised that there were three types of massages; regular, deep tissue and sensual. Officer NOLDER told THOMAS he wanted a sensual massage. THOMAS stated that the sensual massage would be 210.00 dollars, motioned with her hand (indicating manual stimulation) and said "with a happy ending". Officer NOLDER asked what it would cost for "full (meaning full sex)"? THOMAS stated that full service would be 250.00 dollars.

16. At this point Officer NOLDER gave the verbal take down for the vice unit to make entry. Upon entry, THOMAS was taken into custody and the business was secured pending a search warrant.

4

228

REQUESTS

17. Based on the above information, I request the court grant a Search Warrant for the premises known as "S&L Associates" located at 1601 Abbot Road Suite #202 for items listed in attachment "A".

FURTHER YOUR AFFIANT SAITH NAUGHT

Signed under penalty of perjury.

_____	_officer_	_3-4-2010_
Signature	Title	Date

Subscribed and sworn to or affirmed before me on _March 4_, 20_10_, at Anchorage, Alaska.

_____
Judge / Magistrate

5

229

IN THE DISTRICT/SUPERIOR COURT FOR THE STATE OF ALASKA AT ANCHORAGE

☐ STATE ☒ MUNICIPALITY OF ANCHORAGE   CASE NO. 3AN- 10- 8448 ___CR

DEFENDANT Bailey M. Tripp   DOB: 11-6-74   PHONE# 907-315-4342

ORIGINAL CHARGES: Maintaining House of Prostitution

AMENDED CHARGES:

CD# 301	Type of Hearing COP	James PRESENT FOR STATE/MOA	DEFENDANT: Tele.
LOG# 3104	Washington	GL Holmquist PRESENT FOR DEFENDANT	☒ Present ☐ Not Present
DATE 6-15-11	Judge/Magistrate		☐ In-Custody ☒ Not In Custody
TIME 2 AM/PM	Clerk MCalb		

Case initially assigned to Judge ___ Peremptory Challenge Filed By ☐ State/MOA ☐ Defendant Case Reassigned to Judge ___	RIGHTS BY ☐ Video ☐ Court	CRIMINAL RULE 39: ☐ $200 ☐ $250 ☒ Other ___	FINGERPRINTS ☐ Taken ☐ Ordered

PLEA:
☐ Not Guilty   ☐ Guilty   ☐ No Contest
 Cts ___   Cts ___   Cts ___
☒ Dismissal Per Rule 43a Cts ___
PETITION TO REVOKE PROBATION: ☐ Admit ☐ Deny
CRIMINAL RULES 5 & 45: ☐ Runs ☐ Tolled ☐ Rule 45 Expires ___
From ___ to ___

Holmquist - Faller and chief and Pro
This back end of deferred sent against.
5lb dism today
MA - Can pick up cell phone, computer,
ppwk, except for any monies will be pay
Court Case Dism.; Plea withdrawn

BAIL ☐ EXON ☐ FORFEIT ☐ REINSTATE
BAIL   ☐ SET   ☐ CONTINUED
☐ OWN RECOGNIZANCE
☐ CASH APPEARANCE $___
☐ CASH PERFORMANCE $___
☐ CASH/CORPORATE $___
☐ UNSECURED BOND $___
☐ Third-Party Custodian approved

☐ Concurrent w/ ___
CONDITIONS OF RELEASE:
☒ Obey all laws; attend all hearings
☐ Not leave Alaska
☐ No alcohol, illegal drugs
☐ Not possess weapons
☐ No driving w/o valid OL and insurance
☐ No direct or indirect contact w/ ___
☐ Not return to residence of ___

INSTRUCTIONS TO DEFENDANT

Appointment of Counsel. The court has ☐ GRANTED ☐ DENIED your request to have an attorney appointed to represent you. You must contact your attorney within 2 working days from today. If convicted, you will be ordered to pay part of the cost of counsel under Criminal Rule 39. The attorney appointed to represent you is:
☐ Public Defender Agency   ☐ Office of Public Advocacy   ☐ Gorton, Logue & Graper   ☐ Conflict Attorney
   900 W. 5th Ave., Ste. 200   900 W. 5th Ave., Ste. 525   737 M Street   Address: ___
   Phone: 334-4400   Phone: 269-3500   Phone: 276-1945   Phone: ___

THESE ARE YOUR NEXT COURT DATES.
You must appear at all hearings listed below unless your attorney notifies you that you do not need to be present.
A warrant for your arrest will be issued if you fail to appear for any hearing.

Type of Hearing	Date & Time	Type of Hearing	Date & Time
Arraignment		Minor Consuming Alcohol	
Pre-Indictment		Adjudication/Disposition	
Bail Review		Pretrial Conference	
Representation Hearing		Trial Call / Trial	
Change of Plea/Sentencing			
Wellness/Veteran/CRP			
		Report to Jail/Remand	

CR-150 ANCH (5/09)(st.5)
CRIMINAL LOG NOTES

I certify that on this date a copy of this form was given to:
Defendant; Prosecutor; Def's Atty; Calendaring; ASAP; CWS   Clerk: MV

230

IN THE DISTRICT COURT FOR THE STATE OF ALASKA

THIRD JUDICIAL DISTRICT

MUNICIPALITY OF ANCHORAGE,   )
)
                    Plaintiff,   )
)
Vs.   )
)
SHAILEY M. TRIPP,   )
)
                    Defendant.   )
_____)

Case No. 3AN-10-2448 Cr.

ORDER

The court is in receipt of a letter from defendant with attachments

concerning defendant's efforts to secure the return of her property from APD.

The court will treat the letter as a motion and is forwarding a copy of the letter

with attachments to the Municipal Prosecutor's office. The Municipality shall

respond to the motion within 10 days of the date of this order. Plaintiff shall have

5 days to file a reply.

DONE at Anchorage, Alaska this ___30th___ day of November 2011.

PAMELA SCOTT WASHINGTON
DISTRICT COURT JUDGE

I certify that on _11/30/11_ a copy
of the above was mailed to each of the
following at their addresses of record

_____
Administrative Assistant

231

☐ FEL	☒ MISD	☐ NC		MUNICIPALITY OF ANCHORAGE		UCR CODE	CLASS
CROSS-REF #				Anchorage Police Department		CASE NUMBER 10-3748	
				PROPERTY & EVIDENCE REPORT			

TYPE INCIDENT prostitution			☐ ORIGINAL REPORT ☒ SUPPLEMENTAL REPORT	DATE INCIDENT 3/5/10	TIME INCIDENT
LOCATION INCIDENT				DATE REPORTED	TIME REPORTED

CODE	NAME (LAST, FIRST, MIDDLE)	D.O.B.	RACE	SEX	S.S.N.	O.L./STATE
RESIDENCE ADDRESS		HM PHONE	WORK ADDRESS			WK PHONE

A

PROPERTY TAG # 845249	TYPE ARTICLE US currency	CODE	BRAND / MAKE	VALUE 180	EVIDENCE
NCIC NUMBER	MODEL		SERIAL #	SIZE / CALIBER	SAFEKEEP
ENTERED BY	OWNER'S NAME (LAST, FIRST, MIDDLE)		OWNER'S O.L.	OWNER APPLIED #	LOST
DATE ENTERED	OTHER DESCRIPTIVE DATA (COLOR, ACCESSORIES, IF EVIDENCE, LOCATION DISCOVERY):				FOUND
	found in Trinas purse by Padgett -				STOLEN
PROP. LOCATION	Buy $				RECOV'D

B

PROPERTY TAG # 845219	TYPE ARTICLE US currency	CODE	BRAND / MAKE	VALUE 339	EVIDENCE
NCIC NUMBER	MODEL		SERIAL #	SIZE / CALIBER	SAFEKEEP
ENTERED BY	OWNER'S NAME (LAST, FIRST, MIDDLE)		OWNER'S O.L.	OWNER APPLIED #	LOST
DATE ENTERED	OTHER DESCRIPTIVE DATA (COLOR, ACCESSORIES, IF EVIDENCE, LOCATION DISCOVERY):				FOUND
	found in Trinas purse by Padgett				STOLEN
PROP. LOCATION					RECOV'D

C

PROPERTY TAG # 845293	TYPE ARTICLE cell phone	CODE	BRAND / MAKE LG	VALUE	EVIDENCE
NCIC NUMBER	MODEL		SERIAL # mine to get	SIZE / CALIBER	SAFEKEEP
ENTERED BY	OWNER'S NAME (LAST, FIRST, MIDDLE)		OWNER'S O.L.	OWNER APPLIED #	LOST
DATE ENTERED	OTHER DESCRIPTIVE DATA (COLOR, ACCESSORIES, IF EVIDENCE, LOCATION DISCOVERY):				FOUND
	Trinas cell phone - found by Padgett				STOLEN
PROP. LOCATION	Pink + black case				RECOV'D

D

PROPERTY TAG # 845921	TYPE ARTICLE condoms	CODE	BRAND / MAKE	VALUE	EVIDENCE
NCIC NUMBER	MODEL		SERIAL #	SIZE / CALIBER	SAFEKEEP
ENTERED BY	OWNER'S NAME (LAST, FIRST, MIDDLE)		OWNER'S O.L.	OWNER APPLIED #	LOST
DATE ENTERED	OTHER DESCRIPTIVE DATA (COLOR, ACCESSORIES, IF EVIDENCE, LOCATION DISCOVERY):				FOUND
	4 found in office cabinet - Burns				STOLEN
PROP. LOCATION					RECOV'D

NARRATIVE / ADDITIONAL INFO:
seized by search warrant

REPORTING OFFICER	DSN	DATE WRITTEN	SUPERVISOR	DATE	PAGE 1 OF 1

MH100 (Rev. 40/27)

► TYPE INCIDENT			☐ ORIGINAL REPORT	☑ SUPPLEMENTAL REPORT	DATE INCIDENT		TIME INCIDENT
Prostitution					3/11/10		
LOCATION INCIDENT					DATE REPORTED		TIME REPORTED

CODE	NAME (LAST, FIRST, MIDDLE)		D.O.B.	RACE	SEX	S.S.N.		O.L./STATE
RESIDENCE ADDRESS			HM PHONE	WORK ADDRESS				WK PHONE

A PROPERTY TAG #	TYPE ARTICLE		CODE	BRAND / MAKE		VALUE	EVIDENCE
349349	cell phone			Kyocera			EVIDENCE
NCIC NUMBER		MODEL M1000		SERIAL # Transport		SIZE / CALIBER	SAFEKEEP
ENTERED BY	OWNER'S NAME (LAST, FIRST, MIDDLE)			OWNER'S O.L.		OWNER APPLIED #	LOST
							FOUND
DATE ENTERED	OTHER DESCRIPTIVE DATA (COLOR, ACCESSORIES, IF EVIDENCE, LOCATION DISCOVERY)						STOLEN
	Triage cell phone - in waiting room						
PROP. LOCATION	found by						RECOV'D

B PROPERTY TAG #	TYPE ARTICLE		CODE	BRAND / MAKE		VALUE	EVIDENCE
349348	condom wrapper			Life Styles			EVIDENCE
NCIC NUMBER		MODEL		SERIAL #		SIZE / CALIBER	SAFEKEEP
ENTERED BY	OWNER'S NAME (LAST, FIRST, MIDDLE)			OWNER'S O.L.		OWNER APPLIED #	LOST
							FOUND
DATE ENTERED	OTHER DESCRIPTIVE DATA (COLOR, ACCESSORIES, IF EVIDENCE, LOCATION DISCOVERY)						STOLEN
	found in trash can in massage room - Holder						
PROP. LOCATION							RECOV'D

C PROPERTY TAG #	TYPE ARTICLE		CODE	BRAND / MAKE		VALUE	EVIDENCE
349??	condom						EVIDENCE
NCIC NUMBER		MODEL		SERIAL #		SIZE / CALIBER	SAFEKEEP
ENTERED BY	OWNER'S NAME (LAST, FIRST, MIDDLE)			OWNER'S O.L.		OWNER APPLIED #	LOST
							FOUND
DATE ENTERED	OTHER DESCRIPTIVE DATA (COLOR, ACCESSORIES, IF EVIDENCE, LOCATION DISCOVERY)						STOLEN
	Used condom found in trash can in massage room - Holder						
PROP. LOCATION							RECOV'D

D PROPERTY TAG #	TYPE ARTICLE		CODE	BRAND / MAKE		VALUE	EVIDENCE
8							EVIDENCE
NCIC NUMBER		MODEL		SERIAL #		SIZE / CALIBER	SAFEKEEP
ENTERED BY	OWNER'S NAME (LAST, FIRST, MIDDLE)			OWNER'S O.L.		OWNER APPLIED #	LOST
							FOUND
DATE ENTERED	OTHER DESCRIPTIVE DATA (COLOR, ACCESSORIES, IF EVIDENCE, LOCATION DISCOVERY)						STOLEN
PROP. LOCATION							RECOV'D

► NARRATIVE / ADDITIONAL INFO.
See pg 1

REPORTING OFFICER	DSN	DATE WRITTEN	SUPERVISOR		DATE	PAGE 2 OF 6

233

MUNICIPALITY OF ANCHORAGE
Anchorage Police Department
PROPERTY & EVIDENCE REPORT

CROSS-REF #

UCR CODE   CLASS

CASE NUMBER

TYPE INCIDENT _Institution_

☐ ORIGINAL REPORT   ☒ SUPPLEMENTAL REPORT

DATE INCIDENT

TIME INCIDENT

LOCATION INCIDENT

DATE REPORTED

TIME REPORTED

CODE	NAME (LAST, FIRST, MIDDLE)	D.O.B.	RACE	SEX	S.S.N.	O.L./STATE

RESIDENCE ADDRESS   HM PHONE   WORK ADDRESS   WK PHONE

A
PROPERTY TAG # _84303_   TYPE ARTICLE _US currency_   CODE   BRAND / MAKE   VALUE   EVIDENCE

NCIC NUMBER   MODEL   SERIAL #   SIZE / CALIBER   SAFEKEEP

ENTERED BY   OWNER'S NAME (LAST, FIRST, MIDDLE)   OWNER'S O.L.   OWNER APPLIED #   LOST

DATE ENTERED   OTHER DESCRIPTIVE DATA (COLOR, ACCESSORIES, IF EVIDENCE, LOCATION DISCOVERY):   FOUND

PROP. LOCATION   STOLEN

RECOV'D

B
PROPERTY TAG # _84304_   TYPE ARTICLE _computer_   CODE   BRAND / MAKE   VALUE   EVIDENCE

NCIC NUMBER   MODEL   SERIAL #   SIZE / CALIBER   SAFEKEEP

ENTERED BY   OWNER'S NAME (LAST, FIRST, MIDDLE)   OWNER'S O.L.   OWNER APPLIED #   LOST

DATE ENTERED   OTHER DESCRIPTIVE DATA (COLOR, ACCESSORIES, IF EVIDENCE, LOCATION DISCOVERY):   FOUND

PROP. LOCATION   STOLEN

RECOV'D

C
PROPERTY TAG # _84305_   TYPE ARTICLE _Drivers license_   CODE   BRAND / MAKE   VALUE   EVIDENCE

NCIC NUMBER   MODEL   SERIAL #   SIZE / CALIBER   SAFEKEEP

ENTERED BY   OWNER'S NAME (LAST, FIRST, MIDDLE)   OWNER'S O.L.   OWNER APPLIED #   LOST

DATE ENTERED   OTHER DESCRIPTIVE DATA (COLOR, ACCESSORIES, IF EVIDENCE, LOCATION DISCOVERY):   FOUND

PROP. LOCATION   STOLEN

RECOV'D

D
PROPERTY TAG # _84306_   TYPE ARTICLE _papers_   CODE   BRAND / MAKE   VALUE   EVIDENCE

NCIC NUMBER   MODEL   SERIAL #   SIZE / CALIBER   SAFEKEEP

ENTERED BY   OWNER'S NAME (LAST, FIRST, MIDDLE)   OWNER'S O.L.   OWNER APPLIED #   LOST

DATE ENTERED   OTHER DESCRIPTIVE DATA (COLOR, ACCESSORIES, IF EVIDENCE, LOCATION DISCOVERY):   FOUND

PROP. LOCATION   STOLEN

RECOV'D

NARRATIVE / ADDITIONAL INFO:

REPORTING OFFICER   DSN   DATE WRITTEN   SUPERVISOR   DATE   PAGE _3_ OF _6_

| FEL | MISD | NC | | | UCR CODE | CLASS |

CROSS-REF #

CASE NUMBER

| TYPE INCIDENT | | ORIGINAL REPORT | SUPPLEMENTAL REPORT | DATE INCIDENT | | TIME INCIDENT |

LOCATION INCIDENT | DATE REPORTED | TIME REPORTED

| CODE | NAME (LAST, FIRST, MIDDLE) | | D.O.B. | RACE | SEX | S.S.N. | | O.L./STATE |

RESIDENCE ADDRESS | HM PHONE | WORK ADDRESS | WK PHONE

A | PROPERTY TAG # | TYPE ARTICLE *credit card machd* | CODE | BRAND / MAKE *Verifone* | VALUE | EVIDENCE
NCIC NUMBER | MODEL *VX 570* | SERIAL # | SIZE / CALIBER | SAFEKEEP
ENTERED BY | OWNER'S NAME (LAST, FIRST, MIDDLE) | OWNER'S O.L. | OWNER APPLIED # | LOST
DATE ENTERED | OTHER DESCRIPTIVE DATA (COLOR, ACCESSORIES, IF EVIDENCE, LOCATION DISCOVERY) | FOUND
PROP. LOCATION | STOLEN
| RECOV'D

B | PROPERTY TAG # | TYPE ARTICLE *currency* | CODE | BRAND / MAKE | VALUE | EVIDENCE
NCIC NUMBER | MODEL | SERIAL # | SIZE / CALIBER | SAFEKEEP
ENTERED BY | OWNER'S NAME (LAST, FIRST, MIDDLE) | OWNER'S O.L. | OWNER APPLIED # | LOST
DATE ENTERED | OTHER DESCRIPTIVE DATA (COLOR, ACCESSORIES, IF EVIDENCE, LOCATION DISCOVERY) | FOUND
PROP. LOCATION | STOLEN
| RECOV'D

C | PROPERTY TAG # | TYPE ARTICLE *business* | CODE | BRAND / MAKE | VALUE | EVIDENCE
NCIC NUMBER | MODEL | SERIAL # | SIZE / CALIBER | SAFEKEEP
ENTERED BY | OWNER'S NAME (LAST, FIRST, MIDDLE) | OWNER'S O.L. | OWNER APPLIED # | LOST
DATE ENTERED | OTHER DESCRIPTIVE DATA (COLOR, ACCESSORIES, IF EVIDENCE, LOCATION DISCOVERY) | FOUND
PROP. LOCATION | STOLEN
| RECOV'D

D | PROPERTY TAG # | TYPE ARTICLE | CODE | BRAND / MAKE | VALUE | EVIDENCE
NCIC NUMBER | MODEL | SERIAL # | SIZE / CALIBER | SAFEKEEP
ENTERED BY | OWNER'S NAME (LAST, FIRST, MIDDLE) | OWNER'S O.L. | OWNER APPLIED # | LOST
DATE ENTERED | OTHER DESCRIPTIVE DATA (COLOR, ACCESSORIES, IF EVIDENCE, LOCATION DISCOVERY) | FOUND
PROP. LOCATION | STOLEN
| RECOV'D

NARRATIVE / ADDITIONAL INFO.

See pg 1

REPORTING OFFICER | ISN | DATE WRITTEN | SUPERVISOR | DATE | PAGE _____ OF _____

235

MUNICIPALITY OF ANCHORAGE
Anchorage Police Department
PROPERTY & EVIDENCE REPORT

UCR CODE	CLASS
CASE NUMBER	

TYPE INCIDENT		☐ ORIGINAL REPORT ☑ SUPPLEMENTAL REPORT	DATE INCIDENT	TIME INCIDENT
LOCATION INCIDENT			DATE REPORTED	TIME REPORTED

CODE	NAME (LAST, FIRST, MIDDLE)		D.O.B.	RACE	SEX	S.S.N.		O.L./STATE
RESIDENCE ADDRESS			HM PHONE	WORK ADDRESS				WK PHONE

A	PROPERTY TAG #	TYPE ARTICLE		CODE	BRAND / MAKE			VALUE	EVIDENCE
	NCIC NUMBER		MODEL		SERIAL #			SIZE / CALIBER	SAFEKEEP
	ENTERED BY	OWNER'S NAME (LAST, FIRST, MIDDLE)			OWNER'S O.L.		OWNER APPLIED #		LOST
	DATE ENTERED	OTHER DESCRIPTIVE DATA (COLOR, ACCESSORIES, IF EVIDENCE, LOCATION DISCOVERY):							FOUND
	PROP. LOCATION								STOLEN
									RECOV'D

B	PROPERTY TAG #	TYPE ARTICLE		CODE	BRAND / MAKE			VALUE	EVIDENCE
	NCIC NUMBER		MODEL		SERIAL #			SIZE / CALIBER	SAFEKEEP
	ENTERED BY	OWNER'S NAME (LAST, FIRST, MIDDLE)			OWNER'S O.L.		OWNER APPLIED #		LOST
	DATE ENTERED	OTHER DESCRIPTIVE DATA (COLOR, ACCESSORIES, IF EVIDENCE, LOCATION DISCOVERY):							FOUND
	PROP. LOCATION								STOLEN
									RECOV'D

C	PROPERTY TAG #	TYPE ARTICLE		CODE	BRAND / MAKE			VALUE	EVIDENCE
	NCIC NUMBER		MODEL		SERIAL #			SIZE / CALIBER	SAFEKEEP
	ENTERED BY	OWNER'S NAME (LAST, FIRST, MIDDLE)			OWNER'S O.L.		OWNER APPLIED #		LOST
	DATE ENTERED	OTHER DESCRIPTIVE DATA (COLOR, ACCESSORIES, IF EVIDENCE, LOCATION DISCOVERY):							FOUND
	PROP. LOCATION								STOLEN
									RECOV'D

D	PROPERTY TAG #	TYPE ARTICLE		CODE	BRAND / MAKE			VALUE	EVIDENCE
	NCIC NUMBER		MODEL		SERIAL #			SIZE / CALIBER	SAFEKEEP
	ENTERED BY	OWNER'S NAME (LAST, FIRST, MIDDLE)			OWNER'S O.L.		OWNER APPLIED #		LOST
	DATE ENTERED	OTHER DESCRIPTIVE DATA (COLOR, ACCESSORIES, IF EVIDENCE, LOCATION DISCOVERY):							FOUND
	PROP. LOCATION								STOLEN
									RECOV'D

► NARRATIVE / ADDITIONAL INFO:

REPORTING OFFICER	DSN	DATE WRITTEN	SUPERVISOR		DATE	
						PAGE ___ OF ___

236

MUNICIPALITY OF ANCHORAGE
Anchorage Police Department
PROPERTY & EVIDENCE REPORT

UCR CODE   CLASS

CASE NUMBER

TYPE INCIDENT

☐ ORIGINAL REPORT   ☐ SUPPLEMENTAL REPORT

DATE INCIDENT   TIME INCIDENT

LOCATION INCIDENT

DATE REPORTED   TIME REPORTED

CODE   NAME (LAST, FIRST, MIDDLE)   D.O.B.   RACE   SEX   S.S.N.   O.L./STATE

RESIDENCE ADDRESS   HM PHONE   WORK ADDRESS   WK PHONE

A PROPERTY TAG #   TYPE ARTICLE   CODE   BRAND / MAKE   VALUE   EVIDENCE

NCIC NUMBER   MODEL   SERIAL #   SIZE / CALIBER   SAFEKEEP

ENTERED BY   OWNER'S NAME (LAST, FIRST, MIDDLE)   OWNER'S O.L.   OWNER APPLIED #   LOST

DATE ENTERED   OTHER DESCRIPTIVE DATA (COLOR, ACCESSORIES, IF EVIDENCE, LOCATION DISCOVERY):   FOUND

PROP. LOCATION   STOLEN

RECOV'D

B PROPERTY TAG #   TYPE ARTICLE   CODE   BRAND / MAKE   VALUE   EVIDENCE

NCIC NUMBER   MODEL   SERIAL #   SIZE / CALIBER   SAFEKEEP

ENTERED BY   OWNER'S NAME (LAST, FIRST, MIDDLE)   OWNER'S O.L.   OWNER APPLIED #   LOST

DATE ENTERED   OTHER DESCRIPTIVE DATA (COLOR, ACCESSORIES, IF EVIDENCE, LOCATION DISCOVERY):   FOUND

PROP. LOCATION   STOLEN

RECOV'D

C PROPERTY TAG #   TYPE ARTICLE   CODE   BRAND / MAKE   VALUE   EVIDENCE

NCIC NUMBER   MODEL   SERIAL #   SIZE / CALIBER   SAFEKEEP

ENTERED BY   OWNER'S NAME (LAST, FIRST, MIDDLE)   OWNER'S O.L.   OWNER APPLIED #   LOST

DATE ENTERED   OTHER DESCRIPTIVE DATA (COLOR, ACCESSORIES, IF EVIDENCE, LOCATION DISCOVERY):   FOUND

PROP. LOCATION   STOLEN

RECOV'D

D PROPERTY TAG #   TYPE ARTICLE   CODE   BRAND / MAKE   VALUE   EVIDENCE

NCIC NUMBER   MODEL   SERIAL #   SIZE / CALIBER   SAFEKEEP

ENTERED BY   OWNER'S NAME (LAST, FIRST, MIDDLE)   OWNER'S O.L.   OWNER APPLIED #   LOST

DATE ENTERED   OTHER DESCRIPTIVE DATA (COLOR, ACCESSORIES, IF EVIDENCE, LOCATION DISCOVERY):   FOUND

PROP. LOCATION   STOLEN

RECOV'D

NARRATIVE / ADDITIONAL INFO:

REPORTING OFFICER   SSN   DATE WRITTEN   SUPERVISOR   DATE   PAGE

APD-108 (Rev. 4/92)

Municipality of Anchorage

4501 Elmore Road Anchorage, Alaska 99507-1500 Telephone (907) 786-8500 http://www.muni.org

Mayor Dan Sullivan

Anchorage Police Department

OWNER LETTER

SHAILEY TRIPP
28 PARK PLACE DR #1303
COVINGTON LA 70433

Date:	08/25/2011
CASE:	10-3948
Final Claim Date:	09/07/2011

The Anchorage Police Department is in possession of the following disposable property, which our records show you to have an ownership interest. Disposable property not claimed by you will be disposed of in accordance to AMC7.25.030

CALL 786-8660 FOR AN APPOINTMENT!
Appointments to claim property are required. Please call Mon-Thurs 8:00 am to 5:00 pm (except holidays) to schedule an appointment to retrieve your property prior to : 09/07/2011

✓Tag # 843309	DATE BOOK	✓Tag # 843305	BUSINESS CARDS
✓Tag # 843308	LEDGER	✓Tag # 843304	MISC PAPERWORK
✓Tag # 843299	CELL PHONE	✓Tag # 843408	MISC PAPERWORK
✓Tag # 843302	SONY COMPUTER	✓Tag # 843300	LABELS
✓Tag # 843310	NOTEBOOK	✓Tag # 843301	BUSINESS LICENSE
✓Tag # 843296	RECEIPT BOOK		

PLEASE NOTE THE FOLLOWING

- Appointments are mandatory. Appointments may be rescheduled one time.
- Positive Identification is required at the time property is picked up. No exceptions.
- Anchorage Municipal Code 7.25. requires:
  - A signed Indemnity, Defense and Hold Harmless form may be required prior to any release.
  - Any contraband, all drugs, or property illegal to possess are destroyed.
  - All rights or property interests may be forfeited if not claimed by final claim date.
- This may be the only notice you will receive to claim your property without paying a reimbursement fee to the Municipality of Anchorage.

Property will be released during the scheduled appointment at the Anchorage Police Department, 4501 Elmore Road, upon presentation of proper identification and a signed hold harmless form may be required.

Property can be mailed at your expense or released to a third party. (See attached notary form.)

Sincerely,

Amber L. Garrison
Evidence Manager

pg 10 8 le C # 843293 (ce phone pht+black

po 5 y le A # 843311 paperwork

po 4 y le A # 843307 Credit Card machine

Page 1 of 1

Commercial Lease

This Lease is made on the 17 day of August, 2009, by and between Holly Wilson (hereinafter "Landlord") and Shailey M. Tripp dba _Cybertron Corporation + Blue Consultants_ (hereinafter "Tenant"). In consideration for the mutual promises and covenants contained _Shailey Tripp_ herein, and for other good and valuable consideration, the parties hereby agree as follows:

1. The Landlord leases to the Tenant, and the Tenant rents from the Landlord the following described premises 1601 Abbott Road, Unit #202, Anchorage, Alaska, 99507.

2. The term of the Lease shall be for One Year commencing on August 17, 2009, and ending on August 31, 2010.

3. The Tenant shall pay to the Landlord rent of $650.52 a month ($550.00 rent + $100.00 Common Area Charges + $.52 Unit ID Number).

4. The rent is payable in advance (due on the 1st) and mailed to Holly Wilson, 1930 Glenn Highway, Palmer, Alaska, 99645 or deposited into the landlord's bank account:
   First National Bank Alaska
   Account #2350 201 6

5. The Tenant has given a security deposit to the Landlord an amount of $550.00.

6. A late fee of $100.00 will be charged to the Tenant for every month that the Rent is not received by the 5th of the month in which Rent is due and an 18% yearly interest rate will accumulate on all unpaid amounts.

7. The Tenant shall not make any alterations in, additions to or improvements to the premises without the prior written consent of Landlord. The Landlord, at his own expense, shall furnish the following utilities or amenities for the benefit of the Tenant: Gas, Heating, Water & Sewer, Trash Removal, Snow Removal, and Common Area Maintenance.

8. The Tenant, at his own expense, shall furnish the following: Telephone and extra trash removal. Tenant to provide all signage for the business @1601 Abbott Road #202.

239

equipment, phone lines, and plumbing improvements. Tenant will return the space in good working order with reasonable wear and tear excluded.

15. Upon default in any term or condition of this Lease, the Landlord shall have the right to undertake any or all other remedies permitted by Law.

16. This Lease shall be legal binding upon, and inure to the benefit of, the parties, their heirs, successors, and assigns.

Signed this ___18th___ day of ___August___, 20_09_

_____   _____
(Tenant)   Holly Wilson (Landlord)

Emails

Lt. Parker's Email to Shailey Tripp

This email from Lt. Parker of the Anchorage Police department further demonstrates Parker's attitude towards me. In this letter he trivializes the mistakes he made, he belittles me in a derogatory way, and he contradicts himself.

From: DParker@muni.org
To: shaytripp@hotmail.com
CC: MMew@muni.org; SHebbe@muni.org;
JBucher@muni.org; RRyan@muni.org; DKoch@muni.org
Date: Tue, 8 Nov 2011 10:15:30 -0900
Subject: RE: Shailey Tripp

Ms. Tripp,

As I explained in my previous email, all of the items which we seized at your house of prostitution, which were listed as belonging to you, were returned to your attorney-in-fact, Arnuradha K Lawes upon her presentation of your power of attorney on 9-12-11. The only exceptions were the funds which Judge Washington did not order to be returned.
You mention a credit card machine in your e-mail. Today I learned that it was scheduled to be disposed of through auction because there was no owner listed. It is still in Property and if you claim ownership it may be returned to you. Please call (907) 786-8600 to arrange that return. If you have not received all of your property from your attorney-in-fact you should contact her regarding its return. Ms. Lawes signed a receipt for the property which she received from APD on your behalf.
Regarding my press release of January 25, 2011. That release was created to specifically address mischaracterizations of APD's investigation of your prostitution business in the National Inquirer and internet blogs. I have attached a copy for you to review. The release was sent to anyone requesting it and to the national publication which had mischaracterized our investigation. I have corrected telephonically with Ms.

Litman the error in the second bullet point. Initially I contacted detectives in the Vice Unit who recollected the case being initiated through internet advertisement of your prostitution business. Later, I discovered that a report had been taken by a patrol officer from one of your neighboring business. He did some checking on Craigslist and presented the case to the Vice Unit which then did a standard internet prostitution investigation. This factual error was unintentional and insignificant.

APD has never claimed to have examined all of the evidence seized. Your accepting responsibility before the court for your actions negated any further need for examination of the evidence. The paper work evidence was examined and Mr. Palin's name was not found in any of it.

If you have further questions, please feel free to contact me.

Lt. Parker

Lt. Dave Parker
Anchorage Police Department
Public Information Officer
4501 Elmore Road Desk (907) 786-8724
Anchorage, AK 99507 Cell (907) 351-1949

(Note Lt. Parker did attach a copy of the press release to this email)

Email November 29, 2006

Shailey,

Nice to meet you. Thank you for your time.

Todd

Email December 5, 2006

--- On Tue, 12/05/06, <fek9wnr@yahoo.com> wrote:

From: <funinak@gci.net>
Subject: Re: calmness. Thank you so much.
To: "Shay" <alaskapctechy@yahoo.com>
Date: Tuesday, Dec 05, 2006, 1:27 PM

Shay,

I hope this reply gets to you. I am so happy to be there for you. I love the tie! Glad we met and You light up my life,

Todd

----- Original Message -----

From: "Shay" <alaskapctechy@yahoo.com>
Date: Tuesday, Dec 05, 2006 12:40 pm
Subject: calmness. Thank you so much.
To: <funinak@gci.net>

You really are a great listener. I appreciated your insight today and your great gift of calmness you gave to me. Thank you. You really are very special!!!

I feel weird about the other day. Lets keep friendship as friends and professional services professional.

Shay

ps. I hope you liked your tie and don't sweat breakfast.

Get your own web address.
Have a HUGE year through Yahoo! Small Business.

246

Email June 18, 2007

--- On Mon, 06/18/07, S. M. Tripp
<*alaskapctechy@yahoo.com*> wrote:

> From: S. M. Tripp <alaskapctechy@yahoo.com>
> Subject: the talk
> To: "tp" <t.palin@bp.com>
> Date: Monday, October 06, 2007, 10:25 AM
>
> We have to talk. This is too much for me. I need my
> quiet. Thank you for the support but lets cool it. Visit
> your other friends. Yes our friends trust me. Just stop
> ok?
>
> Shay
>
> *tp <t.palin@bp.com>* wrote:
>
> Going to send you a lot of business. Travel a lot
> lately. Things at home tense. Will be by at night at
> regular time. Sending Joe, tom, and a gci friend.
> How are you? Did you go back to school? Was
> happy to see you working the other night. Friends
> seem to like you.
>
>
> Don't let your dream ride pass you by. Make it a
> reality with Yahoo! Autos.

October 19, 2007

--- On Fri, 10/19/07, <*t.ppalin@hotmail.com*> wrote:

From: t.p. <*t.ppalin@hotmail.com*>
Subject: RE: when you feel better write me
something sexy!!
To: "S. M. Tripp" <cybertronsecurity.vpweb@vp.com>
Date: Friday, October 19, 2007, 4:47 PM

oh my, neither can I.

    Date: Fri, 19 Oct 2007 16:42:18 -0700
    From: alaskapctechy@yahoo.com
    Subject: when you feel better
    To: *t.ppalin@hotmail.com*

    I am going to wrap myself around you and
    grind in your lap. I am going to put little
    kisses all over your stomach and thighs. I am
    going to take my tongue and wrap it around
    your balls and take my mouth and cover
    your......
    I can't wait for you to feel better.

    Shay

    Do You Yahoo!?
    Tired of spam? Yahoo! Mail has the best
    spam protection around
    http://mail.yahoo.com

Boo! Scare away worms, viruses and so much more!
Try Windows Live OneCare! Try now!

Email November 28, 2007

--- On Wed, 11/28/07, T.P. <fek9wnr@yahoo.com > , tp
<tpfurrondyak@yahoo.com>wrote:

> From: T.P. <fek9wnr@yahoo.com>
> Subject: RE: reminders....
> To: "S. M. Tripp" <alaskapctechy@yahoo.com>
> Date: Wednesday, November 28, 2007, 11:26 AM

> Fred my friend will be there and I will be there soon!

Email February 10, 2010

--- On Wed, 2/10/10, T P <fek9wnr@yahoo.com
<mailto:fek9wnr@yahoo.com> > wrote:
From: T P <fek9wnr@yahoo.com
<mailto:fek9wnr@yahoo.com> >
Subject: Re: Pictures.
To: "S T" <thankyou_somuch@yahoo.com
<mailto:thankyou_somuch@yahoo.com> >
Date: Wednesday, February 10, 2010, 9:17 PM

Thank you Shailey. I look forward to it!

On 2/10/10, S T <thankyou_somuch@rocketmail.com
<mailto:thankyou_somuch@rocketmail.com> > wrote:

Do you know what FS and GFE are? Or full service escort?
The answer is yes!. I am pretty sure we are talking the same
language.
No worries!!! I will get my stuff together and send it to you.
Kind regards,
Shailey
Ps Did I need to send it to Greg West or you?

Email February 10, 2010 from Todd Palin to Shailey Tripp

--- On Wed, 2/10/10, T P <fek9wnr@yahoo.com
<mailto:fek9wnr@yahoo.com> > wrote:
From: T P <fek9wnr@yahoo.com
<mailto:fek9wnr@yahoo.com> >
Subject: Re: Pictures.
To: "S T" <alaskapctechy@yahoo.com
<mailto:alaskapctechy@yahoo.com> >
Date: Wednesday, February 10, 2010, 8:31 PM

Yes, the slot itself is a legit position (Senior Data Analyst).
The girl we hire will be an employee that gets a paycheck
every two weeks with full company benefits.
What is making you sell your company? It sounds like it
would be lucrative.
Your erotic massage part intrigues me and sets you apart
from some of the other hopefuls. As long someone looks
good, I am willing to give them an interview (this was why I
asked for the body pictures). In the interview is where I ask
the questions you don't ask in email and allow the woman
to "sell herself" as to why she should be hired or why she is
better then everyone else.
Tell me a bit of what you would do during a massage
session. Could you possibly dress up (like you were visiting
a client) with your hair and nails done, and take a picture
like that for me? If I am going to wait 6-8 weeks to hire
someone so that I can talk with you, I want to make sure it
is well worth it (I hope you understand this, due to other
people involved I have to do this formally).
Todd
Ps. I need you to do this for me. I trust you. A lot of money is
riding on this do this for me!

Email Febraury 10, 2010 from Greg West to Shailey Tripp

--- On Wed, 2/10/10, Greg West <gregwestinal@gmail.com
<mailto:gregwestinal@gmail.com> > wrote:
From: Greg West <gregwestinal@gmail.com
<mailto:gregwestinal@gmail.com> >
Subject: Re: Pictures.
To: "S T" <alaskapctechy@yahoo.com
<mailto:alaskapctechy@yahoo.com> >
Date: Wednesday, February 10, 2010, 8:09 PM

The base salary is $80,000 with a VERY nice bonus structure.
Average salary will be $150,000 - $200,000. This position
comes with all company benefits to include health/401K.
He said you would be perfect for this and we know you
need the money.
On 2/10/10, S T <alaskapctechy@yahoo.com
<mailto:alaskapctechy@yahoo.com> > wrote:
Just leave me out of it. I dont need to know anything else.
No. I DO NOT WANT TO.

Email February 25, 2010 from Greg West to Shailey Tripp

Flag this message
Alabama
Thursday, February 25, 2010 10:47 PM
From:
This sender is DomainKeys verified
"Greg West" <gwestinhvl@yahoo.com>Add sender to
Contacts
To:
alaskapctechy@yahoo.com

--- On Thu, 2/25/10, Greg West <gregwestinal@gmail.com>
wrote:

From: Greg West <gregwestinal@gmail.com>
Subject: Re: Pictures.
To: "S T" thankyou_somuch@rocketmail.com, "T P"
funfuninak@yahoo.com, "S H" fek9wnr@yahoo.com
Date: Thursday, February 25, 2010, 10:47 PM

I wanted to send you this. I thought I did before but realize
that I didn't.

We are not an escort company. We are a government
contracting company that has a "different" way of doing
business. The position is a salaried one with a base salary of
$80,000 + full benefits (health, 401K, etc). We also have a
very nice bonus structure that will put that salary well over 6
figures. The clients are higher ranking military government
civilians. We have relationships in many major cities. Our
aquaintance works the circuit with us helping his company
just like me. Basically we work like this, We currently have 3
girls in Los Angeles that we hired back in October for this
venture. We wanted someone local so we wouldn't have to
send every client there. My goal is that my girls will only
work up to 3 days per week. At first, there won't be as many
clients for our local girl, but if it ever gets to a point where
she has more then 4 clients a week consistently, then I will
have to expand. I also want to tell you, since I

253

get asked
this by most candidates, that I hold my interviews at local hotels. I do the interviews in a hotel room for 2 main reasons. The first is that I don't reveal my company to the girl unless I hire you. You wouldn't believe the phone calls I still get from some of the girls I interviewed several months ago. I have to protect my company's name, my clients, my relationship with certain men you know, and my girls. I am sure you can understand. The second reason I choose a hotel room is because of the nature of the interview. I have to make sure I am not talking to law enforcement. You may bring someone with you to the interview but during the actual interview, they can not be in the room. Todd P. has vouched for you, you come highly recommended (redacted)

Email April 14, 2010

Re: Checking in
Wednesday, April 14, 2010 6:03 PM
From:
This sender is DomainKeys verified
"gregwestinal@gmail.com" <gregwestinal@gmail.com>Add
sender to Contacts
To:
"S T" thankyou_somuch@rocketmail.com
No, you are not going to get away with this. I will be
contacting the FBI tomorrow. You can pretend you didn't
do this but I have already proved otherwise. Like I said, hire
yourself a VERY good lawyer. We will not tolerate you. I
have the endorsement of palin himself.

Sent from the Verizon network using Mobile Email

Email Notification of when Todd Palin knew about the
National Enquirer story

From: kristen@(redacted).com <kristen@(redacted).com>
Subject: NEWS!
To: alaskapctechy@yahoo.com
Date: Wednesday, December 15, 2010, 5:32 PM

Hi Shailey,

Alan just called to let me know that they sent a letter to
Todd's lawyer
this morning and gave him until Friday to respond. I think
that Alan
said your name is in the letter but then it sounded like it is
not, so I
will email him to clarify. If anyone contacts you, he wants
to know.
You can tell me and I can let him know. I hope this is good
news. Call
me if you want to. I will be in touch soon. Sweet dreams?

The Others

This is a list of names of men and women I met through Todd who performed sexual acts for money. Most likely these are not their real names.

Andie
Carla Fisher
Cindy Rausa
Dawn Marie
Eric J.
Josh M.
L. Smith
Steve M.

The Clients

These are the names of clients who I can remember who actually used their real names.

Anthony Nelson
Brian Yager
Daryl Luo
Greg West
John Lowber
Max Easley
Mike Utsler
Padgett
Ron Duncan

Epilogue

When I was a little girl and in high school, never in a million years would I have ever thought my life would have turned out the way it did. When I was sixteen and in my early twenties I truly thought I was going to be a rocket scientist, a pilot, or an astronaut. If anyone would have ever told me I was going to be a prostitute I would have laughed at them.

When the National Enquirer came out with my story my family got calls from India and England less than twenty four hours after it hit the news stands. The power of the media is clearly incredible. The pain and shock my family experienced I can not pretend to imagine. The hurt and let down was great. I had always been the black sheep of the family but now my place was solidified. But an incredible thing happened after the shock. A place of healing has started. It is not perfect but we as a family are starting to heal.

Writing this book was one of the hardest things I have ever done. It was embarrassing, painful and humiliating. I felt naked and exposed. However, through this process I have been able to clearly see the mistakes that I made. It has been cathartic for me and a way for me to heal. It was similar to the way I felt after my first interview with the National Enquirer and after I began writing my blog. I started shedding weight, and I began sleeping better.

My life is not perfect now. Money is still a real problem. I dream of going back to school and completing the degree I almost finished in Anchorage. I want that perfect job. One with health benefits and a schedule that will allow me to tend to my children and their needs. My kids are still handicapped but our life is much more manageable than it ever was before. We live where the weather is warm and sunny most of the year and we are now close to family and friends who love us unconditionally.

I still have my fights and battles. I am in an ongoing struggle with the Anchorage Police Department. Parker's actions and the police still need to be accountable for not returning all of my property and for issuing a false press release. I battle with the media, trying to get them to even look at the evidence I have and the depth of the story I am offering. Even media sources such as Hustler magazine and ashleymadison.com have steered cleared of me. After what Geoffrey Dunn went through I can understand why people stay away from me.

I am currently trying to get help from lawyers, the ACLU, and other sources to help me navigate the finer points with all of the entities that have been hiding my story and releasing false information about me. In addition Ed Opperman, a forensics expert and private investigator, has many of my materials returned from the APD for review and investigation. These materials-electronic & paper-further help support my story.

I have no more secrets. I have a sense of who I am now. I feel like I have so much to offer to the world, my children and my family. My mind is as sharp as ever.

I am dealing with all the abuse I have experienced in my life and learning to be a better parent. I am learning to manage the daily stress in my life so I am not constantly in survival mode. When I wake up in the mornings I actually feel excited about the day ahead and just getting dressed is no longer a major source of stress.

But most importantly I have no more secrets. I have a sense of who I am now. I feel like I still have so much to offer to the world and to my children and my family. My mind is as sharp as ever. I am dealing with all the abuse in my life and learning to be a better parent. I am learning to mange the daily stress in my life so I am not constantly in survival mode. When I wake up in the mornings I actually feel excited about it.

This journey is not over. I am still paying for all the mistakes I made. My struggles are still harsh and real but I have support, love, and God in my life now. I am learning to give love and receive love. I am learning to steer away from drama. It is a learning process. I still slip and make mistakes. The difference is I don't try to hide them now. I can reach out for help and have people in my life who will help me.

As for my relationship with my parents, that is a work in progress. We are making headway. I love my parents very much. I know they love me. They, too, came from difficult backgrounds and they are learning, as well. They are wonderful grandparents. We still have many disagreements but we do want to work through our issues. We all want to change. I think this is real progress of which we are all proud.

Lastly I hope that any man, woman, child, teenager who has become a prostitute will gain hope and courage. Even now, there are times when I think, God I could go out right now and do a hand job and buy groceries. I know what that feels like; I know how high the temptation is.

If you are in this situation, seek help. There are shelters, churches and other organizations that will provide assistance. Perhaps you can't go to the authorities or to the media but you can change. I hope you find the strength within to do that for yourself. The greatest gift I received through all of this chaos was self-love. I want that for others in situations similar to mine, too.

As for me right now in this moment, I hope that this book will be successful and help me support my family. I hope that I will be able to complete my education. And I hope to continue to grow in my art, my writing, and my spirituality. I am already branching out and have started work on a children's book. Lastly, I hope to make contributions in the world with all my ideas in the sciences. I want my children to grow up happy, safe, and confident.

What more can I ask?

Acknowledgements

This book could not have been written without the unconditional support and love of my family and close friends.

A special thank you to Vickie Bottoms for helping me stay in the moment and keep me honest. For never giving up. For being so dedicated to see this project through to the end and for believing in me and our partnership in writing this book.

Thank you to my astounding and hardworking editors Allison from thepalinplace.blogspot.com, Enid Dunn, and those of you who wish to remain unnamed. You really came through for me. You encouraged me and inspired me. No words can say how much I appreciate you. You made me laugh and kept me real.

I want to thank all the people who believed in me and encouraged me to write this book. Again many wish to be anonymous but thank you anyway. A special thank you to Malia Litman, Jesse Griffin, and other blogs for writing about me and giving me an opportunity to respond.

Thank you Ed Opperman. Your patience, kindness, guidance, and prayers will forever have touched my life. You helped me in many ways just by being there in the background and for giving me positivity at the times I felt all alone in this endeavor. Thank you for all your hard work.

A shout out to Mom, & Dad. A special thanks to Pink Hat Productions and all the people I have met through them.

Helpful Information

The National Domestic Violence Helpline
  1-800-799-SAFE(7233) or **TTY 1-800-787-3224.**

The National Parent Helpline
  1-855- 4A PARENT • 1-855-427-2736

The National Suicide Prevention Hotline
  1-800-273-8255